1 MONTH FREE READING

at

www.ForgottenBooks.com

By purchasing this book you are eligible for one month membership to ForgottenBooks.com, giving you unlimited access to our entire collection of over 1,000,000 titles via our web site and mobile apps.

To claim your free month visit: www.forgottenbooks.com/free849525

* Offer is valid for 45 days from date of purchase. Terms and conditions apply.

English
Français
Deutsche
Italiano
Español
Português

www.forgottenbooks.com

Mythology Photography **Fiction**
Fishing Christianity **Art** Cooking
Essays Buddhism Freemasonry
Medicine **Biology** Music **Ancient Egypt** Evolution Carpentry Physics
Dance Geology **Mathematics** Fitness
Shakespeare **Folklore** Yoga Marketing
Confidence Immortality Biographies
Poetry **Psychology** Witchcraft
Electronics Chemistry History **Law**
Accounting **Philosophy** Anthropology
Alchemy Drama Quantum Mechanics
Atheism Sexual Health **Ancient History**
Entrepreneurship Languages Sport
Paleontology Needlework Islam
Metaphysics Investment Archaeology
Parenting Statistics Criminology
Motivational

OXBURGH HALL, NORFOLK.

Bedingfelds of Oxburgh

BY

CATHERINE BEDINGFELD

PRIVATELY PRINTED

1912

OXBURGH HALL, NORFOLK.

The Bedingfelds of Oxburgh

BY

KATHERINE BEDINGFELD

PRIVATELY PRINTED

1912

PREFACE

IN printing these simple notes from the records of an ancient house, the compiler wishes to make her grateful acknowledgments to Sir Henry Bedingfeld, who most generously placed all the family papers at her disposal, to Mr. E. M. Beloe, for his kind permission to quote from his father's learned paper on Oxburgh, and to reproduce his own map of the neighbourhood, and to the Rev. Father O'Donohoe, S.J., for help in revising her MS. and reading the proofs.

March 1912.

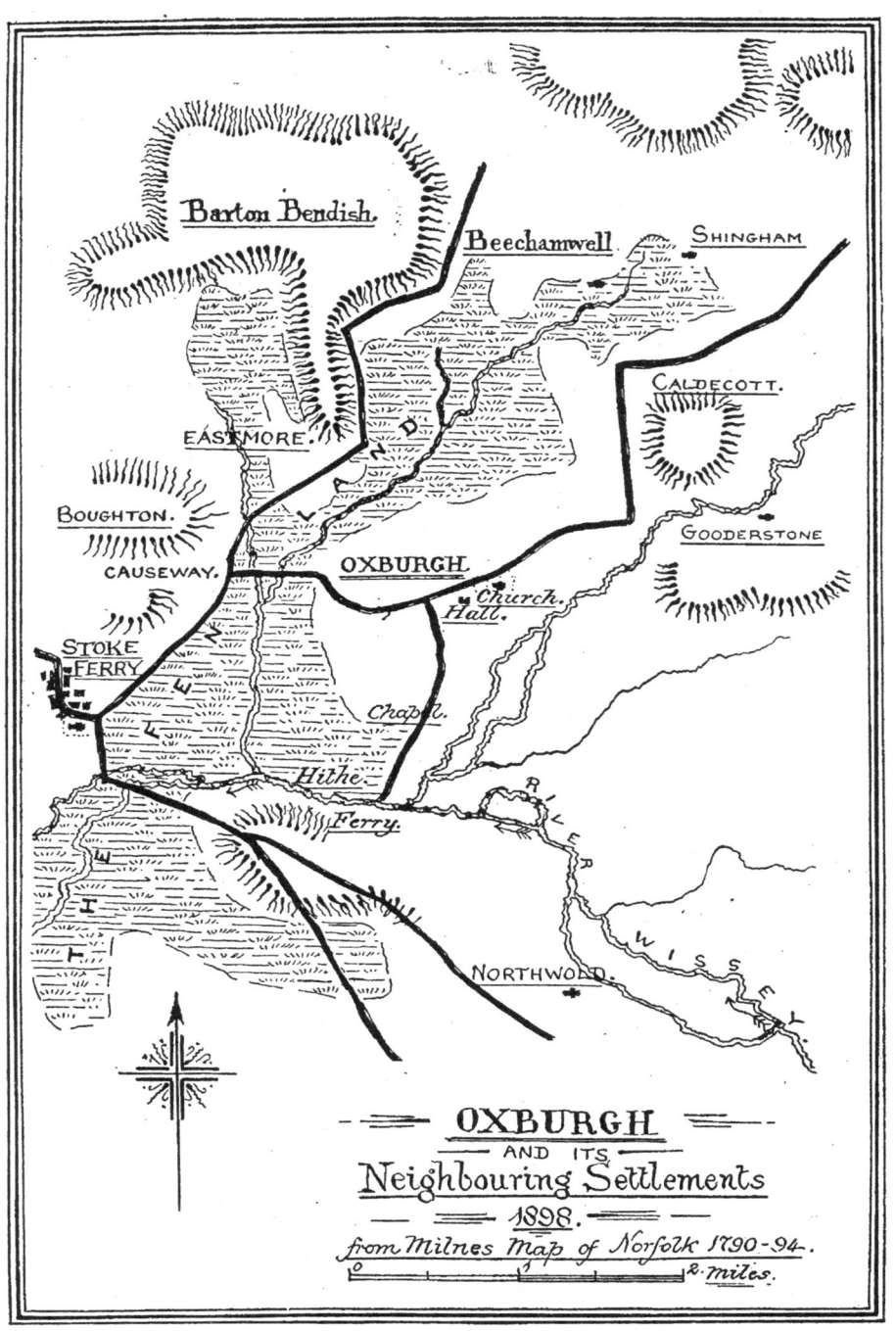

REPRODUCED HERE BY THE KIND PERMISSION OF
MR. E. M. BELOE.

The Bedingfelds of Oxburgh.

PART I.

THE KNIGHTS OF THE FAMILY.

M.LXVI.—M.DC.LVII.

OXBURGH stands on a promontory stretching into the great fen. Its name may imply a fort. Its central position, commanding as it does a great tract of country behind it, was chosen by our early forefathers as a place of strength and protection. The fens come close up to the higher land on which Oxburgh stands. To the north an arm of the fenland goes inland, extending eastward some two or three miles to Shingham, and the passage from the opposite promontory at Stoke to the settlement at Oxburgh is at the entrance of this kind of gulf, over which the road is carried on a dam and bridge. The causeway is some half a mile long, and on either side of the road it still is little better than a lake full of water.

Thus the fen runs up past the promontory to the north. Southward the stream comes down from the hill forming its protection on that side, and it is by this southern boundary that the earlier settlement appears to have been. Within this promontory, which was chosen for its natural defence, the land was covered with the remains of the life of early settlers. To the north-west was the trench, to the south-west were the tumuli, and those curious depressions of the earth which until recent times were called Danes' graves, and by the side of what now is the rectory is the chapel, which marks probably the site of the older borough, and around which for acres are found the remains of many hundreds of those that were buried there. At the back, on the east side, runs the ancient way over Langwade—the Long Ford—and beside it the ancient Cross still called the Langer (Langwade) Cross.

Nothing is left of the early history of Oxburgh and its neighbouring settlements, except what is written in the names of the villages near it, showing their settlements on the beach or on the well[1], or, as Stoke on the opposite shore of the northern gulf, the fortification by the water, and except what is scarred on the land by its dykes or raised by its tumuli and forts.

In its territorial rights, and also in its business, Oxburgh was a great place, and had its harbour near the older settlement by the rectory. It is still called the Hythe, and up to within the last century there were large warehouses there, and ships came backwards and forwards, taking the corn and bringing back merchandise to the district.[2]

In *Domesday Book* the place is called Oxenburgh, a

---

[1] Beach signifies the shore of the fen, as in Waterbeach and Wisbeach; the great fen, especially where there was most water, was called the well. Both words are seen in Beechamwell.
[2] Edward M. Beloe, F.S.A. (Written in A.D. 1890).

name taken from its site on the Ouse or Wissey, and this name it very well answers, as being a peninsula surrounded by two or three rivulets; the adjunct burgh bespeaks its eminence, showing it to have been some fortified town or place of strength, and about half-a-mile from the town, on a place called the Warren Hill, may be seen a deep vallum or trench. The word burgh may also mean some place of burial. Oxburgh was a place of account in the time of the Romans, some of Constantine's coins having been discovered there; and in the time of the Danes it was in Royal hands, Canute having made Turchill, one of their chief leaders, lord of the town. He held it through St. Edward the Confessor's time, but William the Conqueror gave it to his own nephew, Ralph de Limesi, a Norman baron.[1]

I now come to the history of the family which has been connected with Oxburgh for so many centuries, so closely bound up indeed with it that it seems impossible to speak of one without the other.

The founder of the family of Bedingfeld was Ogerus de Pugeys, a Norman knight, who came to England with the Conqueror. He was one of the four knights of the Lord Malet, Lord of the Honour of Eye in Suffolk, who gave him the Manor of Bedingfeld in that county, from which he assumed the name now enjoyed by his descendants.

The component parts of this name are apparently Saxon, but these, viz., Beding (a bed or couch), and Feld (a field), by no means afford a satisfactory etymology.

[1] Blomefield's *History of Norfolk*.

The son and successor of Ogerus de Pugeys, Peter de Bedingfeld, with the consent of Arnold his son, by a deed about the year 1156, gave the advowson of the church of Bedingfeld to the Prior and Convent of Snapes in Suffolk.

His son, Arnold de Bedingfeld, of whom we have just made mention, lived in the reign of Henry II., and by his wife Orframnia was father of three sons[1] (1) Gerard de Bedingfeld, who died without issue,[2] (2) Sir Adam, (3) Silvester, father of a son Walter, who was witness to a deed of donation to Snape Priory about 1170. Sir Adam de Bedingfeld had a contest with Egevine, Abbot of Snape Priory, concerning some land, about the year 1210. He married Maria Gundreda, widow of Robert de Malwell, by whom he had Adam de Bedingfeld, whose son, Sir Peter de Bedingfeld, Knight, was succeeded by his son, Sir Adam de Bedingfeld, Knight, 1245, whose son, Sir Adam de Bedingfeld, Knight, was steward of the Honour of Eye.[3] This Sir Adam had a daughter Roesia, wife of John de Hoo, and a son, Sir Peter de Bedingfeld, Knight, who left two sons, viz., Sir Edmund, and James, ancestor of the Bedingfelds of

---

[1] This Arnold de Bedingfeld and Orframnia his wife sold to Robert de Thorp, of Thorp Abbots, in Norfolk, 2 messuages, a mill, 120 acres of land, 4 of meadow, and 10 of wood in 1171, at Thorp Abbots.

[2] This Gerard de Bedingfeld, son of Arnold, lived in the reign of Richard I. Sampson, Abbot of Bury, gave him land at Bedingfeld. (This Abbot Sampson lives again in the pages of Carlyle's *Past and Present*).

[3] This last named Sir Adam de Bedingfeld in 1276 sealed with the family arms *Erm* an eagle displayed *gul* (Blomefield). He is frequently mentioned in the Hundreds Roll 3 Edward I. as Seneschal of the Honour of Eye. According to another authority *his* father, Adam de Bedingfeld sealed with the family arms in 1245.

Ditchingham, in Norfolk. Sir Peter died before 1299, and was succeeded by Sir Edmund de Bedingfeld, Knight, who married Maud, daughter and heiress of Sir William Hemenhale, Knight. This lady, after Sir Edmund's death, became the wife of Sir Richard de Amoundville and died in 1323. Sir Edmund, by his wife, Maud, had a son, Peter de Bedingfeld, who married Margaret, daughter of Thomas Bacon, Esq., and died in 1371. Sir Peter's will was proved in this same year; he bequeathed his body to be buried in the churchyard of St. Mary of Bedingfeld, and left money for the making of a window in that church before the altar of St. James and for a new porch. The will was dated at Bedingfeld. The will of Margaret, his wife, was proved in 1380, and she willed to be buried in the church of Bedingfeld. There is a grant of Edward III. at Oxburgh to this Sir Peter, with the great seal annexed. It is as follows:

"Edward by the grace of God, King of England and France and lord of Ireland: To all baylies and faithful subjects, greeting.

Know ye that whereas Peter de Bedingfeld, Chevaler, convened before us in our chancery Roger de Wurstgate and Gilbert de Debenham, of the county of Suffolk, his detainers, concerning coming to us in the parts beyond seas, in (company) of our beloved and faithful Hugo de Dudell, Count of Gloucester, or other peers appointed for the expedition of our wars beyond the seas, in the next passage to those parts, and remaining there during our pleasure, at his own proper charges, We, willing to show especial favour to the aforesaid

Peter, from all homicide, felony, robberies, larcenies, by the said Peter, committed, however he may stand accused, We grant him our firm peace: so nevertheless that he march, in our next passage aforesaid, to the parts aforesaid, and remain there in our service at his own proper charges as aforesaid; and when he returns from thence, We will that his accuser be directly in our court to plead against him concerning the homicides, felonies, robberies, and larcenies aforesaid.

> Witness : Edward Duke of Cornwall, and Count of Chester, our beloved son, Custos of England.
>
> Given at Cloft the 8th day of October the 16th of our reign of England, and of France the 3rd. Edward the III. Oct. 8, 1343."[1]

This Sir Peter's son, Sir Thomas Bedingfeld, Knight, living in the reign of Henry IV., married Elizabeth de Norton, of Rendham and Norton, near Woolpit, in Suffolk. His son, Sir Thomas de Bedingfeld, living in the reign of Henry V., was father of Edmund de Bedingfeld, Esq., who married Margaret, daughter of Sir Robert Tuddenham. By her he obtained (besides many others) the lordship of Oxburgh, henceforth the principal residence of himself and his successors. Margaret was a great heiress, as shown forth in her will, dated at Ereswell, May 24th, 1474. She bequeathed her body to be buried before the image

---

[1] This grant is endorsed as revised by the King at Southwark in Michaelmas term two years later. (Rolls 66, among the placita of the Crown.)

of the Holy Cross, near the altar of the Blessed Virgin, in the nave of the Church of St. Peter, of Ereswell; forty pounds for vestments, books, and necessary ornaments, and to the repair of the said church; fifty-three shillings and four pence for a vestment, in which her chantry priest was to officiate on high festivals, before the altar of the Blessed Virgin. To St. Lawrence's Chapel at Ereswell, fifty-three shillings and four pence; ten marks to the poor dwelling in her Manor of Ereswell; an house with gardens, pastures, meadow grounds, and forty-two acres of land, with liberty of salvage, for a chantry priest to officiate daily in the Church of St. Peter for her soul, and that of her father, mother, grandfather, grandmother, husband, children, brother, etc.; to the Monastery of Brusyard, in Suffolk, where her mother was buried, one hundred shillings, and to the Augustine Friars, in London, where her brother Thomas was buried, twenty pounds; desiring that a good and decent marble stone should be bought to cover his body, and that the residue should be divided amongst the friars there. To the church of Bedingfeld, where her husband was buried, forty-six shillings and eight pence for a vestment, in memory of her and her husband. Other bequests follow, to the Friars Minor at Babewell, the Carmes at Ipswich, the Friars Preachers at Thetford, the Augustine Friars and the nuns there. To the repair of Bedingfeld nunnery, ten shillings. A silver cup to the altar of the Blessed Virgin at Ereswell. To every priest attending at Mass on the day of her sepulture, eightpence; and to the Lady Alice Tuddenham (her sister), a nun at

Crab House, ten marks. The will of her husband, Edmund Bedingfeld, is dated at Bedingfeld in 1446, the twenty-fourth year of Henry VI.[1] He was succeeded by his son, Thomas Bedingfeld, Esq., who married Anne, daughter and heiress of John de Waldegrave, Esq., by whom he had a son, Edmund, his successor. Thomas Bedingfeld died on October 12th, 1453, in Northampton, his aforesaid son Edmund being only ten years old. Thomas was buried at Waldegrave. The will of Anne his wife is dated 1453. She desired to be buried in the churchyard of Bedingfeld, by the porch which was built over Sir Peter's body (great-great-grandfather of her husband).

I now come to Edmund Bedingfeld, who was left fatherless at the age of ten, of whom Alice, Duchess of Suffolk, by her deed dated December 1st, 1454, granted the custody and wardship, to his great uncle, Sir Thomas Tuddenham. This Edmund was destined to be the builder of the famous old towers and moated castle at Oxburgh, which has been the residence of his descendants ever since in an unbroken line. In the year 1482, July 3rd, Edmund Bedingfeld had a royal patent from King Edward IV. to build the present manor house of Oxburgh with towers, battlements, etc., "more castelli," and for a weekly Mercate in this town, on Friday, with a pye powder court to be kept by the steward or bailiff of the said Mercate. "This

---

[1] He bequeaths his body to be buried in the churchyard of Bedingfeld, gives to Margaret his wife all the goods and chattels which Margaret Tuddenham (daughter of John Herling, Esq.) had given her. To Thomas, his son and heir, twelve silver spoons and a covered cup, which was his father's, and to his little grandson Edmund, son and heir of his son Thomas, a silver cup.

ancient seat[1] stands a little south-west of the church of Oxburgh, being built of brick; it very much resembles Queens' College in Cambridge, built also in the same reign. The present entrance to it is over the bridge of brick with three great arches, and embattled with freestone (formerly over one of wood, with its drawbridge), through a grand majestick tower, the arch whereof is about 22 feet long and 13 broad; to this tower adjoin four turrets, one at each corner, like the tower, of brick, coped also and embattled with freestone, projecting and octangular; the two in front are about 80 feet or more from the foundation in the moat to the summit, and about 10 feet above the great tower. The courtyard (about which stands the house) is 118 feet long and 92 broad; opposite to the great tower on the south side of the court stands the hall, in length about 54 feet and 34 in breadth; between the two bow-windows, the roof is of oak (in the same style and form as that of Westminster), equal in height to the length of it, and being lately very agreeably ornamented and improved, may be justly accounted one of the best old Gothick halls in England. The outward walls of the house stand in the moat, which is pure running water (fed by an adjoining rivulet) about 270 feet long and 52 broad on every side, and faced with brick on the side opposite to the house, and can be raised to the depth of 10 feet of water or let out, as occasion serves."

In the tower on the right hand of the entrance is a spiral staircase of brick leading to the top. It is lighted by small quatrefoil apertures. The other tower

[1] Blomefield, *History of Norfolk*, 1807.

is divided into four stories, three of which have groined brick ceilings, with projecting ribs. The chamber in the centre and over the entrance is spacious, having a large mullioned window to the north, and two bay windows to the south, looking into the court: it is curiously paved with small fine bricks, and the walls are hung with tapestry representing many figures of the time of Edward IV. This tapestry is remarkable, and is considered an heirloom, being mentioned in many of the old family wills.

In a turret projecting from the east tower is a small closet in the solid wall, measuring 6 feet long by 5, and 7 feet high, entered by a trap door concealed in the pavement. It may well have been used as a priest's "hiding hole" in the penal times following the Reformation, but it evidently existed before that time, and is probably coeval with the house itself.[1]

Edmund Bedingfeld married twice, first Alice, daughter of Sir Ralph Shelton, Knight, by whom he had a daughter, Margaret, who became the wife of Edward Jernegan of Suffolk, and secondly Margaret, daughter of Sir John Scot, or Oscott, of Scot's Hall, Kent, by whom he had four sons and two daughters. She died in 1514; by her will, dated January 12, 1513, she bequeathed her body to be buried in the church of Oxburgh, before the image of the Trinity, and was the foundress of a chapel there. She gave to the Gilds of the Holy Trinity, St. Thomas, and Corpus Christi, 6s. 8d. each (these were the Oxburgh guilds) and legacies to the high altars of several of the neighbouring churches.

[1] In the dungeon an interesting pre-Reformation rosary was found.

ENTRANCE TO THE DUNGEON IN THE EAST TOWER, OXBURGH.

The sons and daughters of Edmund and his second wife, Margaret, were as follows. (1) Sir Thomas, married first Margaret Clifford, secondly Alice, daughter of William London. (2) Robert, a priest.[1] He was pensioner of Corpus Christi College in Cambridge, where he gave the west windows of the building leading from the College to Bennet church. He was Rector of Ereswell and Oxburgh, and was buried at Oxburgh, July 1st, 1539. (3) Edmund. (4) Peter, lord of Quidenham,[2] who was married twice; by his second wife, who was daughter of John Morings[3] of Greynford in Kent, he had John Bedingfeld, his son and heir, who married Alice, daughter of Humphrey Kervile, of Wigenhall St. Maries, who outlived him, and married Sir John Sulyard, Knight. John Bedingfeld died on January 1st, 1545. At his death he held Quidenham Manor and Advowson of the Duke of Norfolk, as of Kenninghall Manor, by fealty, &c., and also 100 acres of land and pasture in Quidenham called Chamberlains, held of Thos. Tirrell Knt. as of Banham by fealty and 44s. rent, and also of Hocham Parva

---

[1] There is amongst the post-Reformation papers at Oxburgh one concerning this Robert Bedingfeld, who besides being Rector of Oxburgh and Ereswell, also held the living of Caysterton in the Lincoln diocese. In this paper, which is evidently a renewal of the Papal Licence, the King grants to Robert Bedingfeld the full effect of the Bull received from Rome in 1512. It is dated 1537, in the 29th year of Henry VIII.'s reign. The great seal attached is in good preservation.

Robert Bedingfeld was therefore exercising his priestly functions in the troubled and perplexing period that followed the King's divorce from Queen Catherine of Aragon.

[2] Peter Bedingfeld had Quidenham from his father Sir Edmund Bedingfeld, Knight of the Bath, in right of the heiress of the Tuddenhams.

[3] Sometimes spelt Morings and sometimes Moninges.

Manor, &c.[1] His son Humphrey Bedingfeld became lord; he married Margaret, daughter of Edward Cocket of Ampton, by whom he had two daughters, viz., Dorothy and Frances. The latter, on the death of her sister, became sole heiress, and married Anthony Thwaite, of Hardyngham, whose only daughter and heiress, Elizabeth, married Jeffrey Cobb, of Sandringham, whose son, William Cobb, of Sandringham, was living in 1664.

Of Edmund Bedingfeld's two daughters one, Alice, was married to Sir Philip Booth, Knight.

The account I have given of Oxburgh Hall is taken from the pages of Blomefield, and was written about the year 1749, before the ill-fated time when Sir Edmund's descendant, Sir Richard Bedingfeld, pulled down the magnificent old hall on the south side of the mansion, in the year 1778. Edmund Bedingfeld was created a Knight of the Bath at the coronation of Richard III., and the King also gave him permission to use the Badge of the Fetterlock. Sir Edmund being a firm adherent of the House of York, this privilege was probably given as a mark of favour, and of his attachment to the cause.

From an old inventory of Oxburgh it was found that one room was called by the name of the "Fetterlock Room."

Sir Edmund was the first male of his line to hold Oxburgh, and he built the hall eight years after he came there. His first wife was Alice Shelton, and Mr. Beloe thinks that Sir Edmund used Shelton Hall (built a little earlier than Oxburgh, probably by Ralph

[1] Blomefield.

THE "KING'S ROOM," OXBURGH.
TAPESTRY WORKED BY MARY QUEEN OF SCOTS AND LADY SHREWSBURY.

MARY QUEEN OF SCOTS
(*From a portrait at Oxburgh.*)

Shelton) as a model in building his own house. He might have wished that his wife, Alice, should have in Oxburgh a memory of her old home. (Mr. Beloe had seen a perfect drawing of Shelton Hall, and was able to compare the two places.)

It is thought that Sir Edmund must have rendered some good service to Henry VII., as that King (usually so sparing of his favours) paid him a visit at Oxburgh, the room where he lodged being called the King's room to this day, and conferred on him several lordships in Yorkshire. The Royal visit happened in this wise. The King was travelling in Norfolk in 1497 with the Queen, and his mother the Countess of Derby. They went to Walsingham on pilgrimage, and arrived at Lynn accompanied by a large retinue of nobles, and the Bishops of London and Bath. The party went on to Oxburgh from Lynn, and stayed at Oxburgh several days. The Queen was probably lodged in the room over the King's room, as it is known by the name of the Queen's Room.

Sir Edmund made his will at Calais, on the 12th October, 1496, and it was proved the 28th January following. He bequeathed his body to be buried in the church of Oxburgh, before the Holy Trinity, and gives £40 to lead the church of Caldecote.[1]

The church of Oxburgh was dedicated to St. John

---

[1] Allusion has been made to the church which used to stand near the rectory at Oxburgh. Blomefield describes it as the ancient parochial or mother church, being a single building of flint ... a very plain rude edifice about 34 feet in length and 20 in breadth, very much resembling the church at Glastonbury said to be built by Joseph of Arimathea. A Saxon coin was dug up here of Eldred, who was King of England in 946, about whose reign this church was most likely erected.

the Evangelist, and founded about the reign of Edward I. There was a chantry attached in honour of the Holy Trinity, the glorious Virgin Mary, St. John the Evangelist, and All Saints. It was well endowed with seventeen acres of pasture enclosed, seven score and five acres, with three roods of arable land. The house belonging to the chantry in which the priest lived, stood in the town of Oxburgh, a little east of the church, being a great building, and had lately[1] a large hall, with screens, butteries, etc., enclosed next the street, with a lofty wall of freestone with embattlements of the same. The entrance to it was through a neat and lofty arch in the walls, now bricked up. (Some of this is still remaining in 1912). The Abbot of West Dereham held here, in the reign of Henry III., "the third part of the fourth of a fee." The Abbey was taxed in 1428 for their temporalities at Oxburgh.[2]

At one time there were seven guilds in this parish, as may be seen by the will of one of the parish priests, John Gardener, 1470, who was buried in St. John the Evangelist's Church before the image of St. Paul—"To

---

[1] The account is taken from Blomefield.

[2] The following is taken from a document at Oxburgh, inscribed, Foundation of the Chantry at Oxburgh:

Willelmus Shympling, Chantorie prest (presbyter) Thos Hawar, Johannes Curlington, Church wardens. They certify that their is in the said towne a chanterie wh. was founded by Richard Sparrowe to fynde a prest to sing in the Church of Oxburgh, to pray et reliqua, of which said chanterie the said Willelmus Shympling is now incumbent, a man of indifferent lernyng, and good conversation having no other living but the same the hole proffytts of which said chanterie have been employed to the use of the said prest continually untill this present day.

A CORNER IN THE BEDINGFELD CHAPEL SHOWING
SOME OF THE TERRA-COTTA WORK NOW
WHITEWASHED.

keep up the green torches, 2s.; to the guilds of Corpus Christi, Holy Trinity, St. Mary, St. John the Baptist, and St. Peter, two shillings each. All Saints, and St. Thomas the Martyr, 12d. each." The beautiful chapel of freestone in the east end of the south aisle was founded by Margaret Bedingfeld, relict of Sir Edmund. By her will, dated 12th January, 1513, she bequeathed her body to be buried in the church of Oxburgh, before the image of the Trinity, "where I will a chapel to be erected." The tomb at the east end is of terra cotta, and in the renaissance style, probably foreign work.

About two miles east of the town, on the road to Cley, a little before you come to Langwade Cross (part of which is still standing), on the green way, which is the boundary between Oxburgh and Cley, was a house of lepers. Thomas Salmon, chaplain of Oxburgh in 1380, gave by will to the Chapel of St. Mary at Oxburgh three shillings and fourpence, and to the lazars at Langwade 6d. There was an ancient family who took their name from the longwade or passage here over the river.

Sir Edmund's eldest son, Sir Thomas, died without issue, and Robert, the second son, was in holy orders, so the inheritance descended to Edmund, the third son. He attended Henry VIII. in his wars abroad, and was knighted by Charles Brandon, Duke of Suffolk, and General of the English army, for his bravery, at Montdedier in France, at the taking of that town in 1523. Sir Edmund married Grace, daughter of Lord Marney (the portrait of the latter is at Oxburgh in the north library). They had five sons and two daughters, viz., (1) Henry, his successor, (2) Francis, who married a daughter of John Wodehouse, (3) Anthony, who married Elizabeth, daughter and heiress of Sir Roger Danyells, (4) Humphrey, who married Mary, daughter of John Earle, Esq., and (5) Edmund, who married Mary, daughter and heiress of John Russell, by whom he had four sons, John, Edmund, Daniel, and Humphrey. The latter, Humphrey, was employed by his uncle to ascertain the state of the country and the opinions of the people concerning the levies made for the service of Queen Mary. His wife's name was Hicks, and he had two sons, (1) Daniel, (2) Christopher. With regard to his brother Edmund, in May, 1557, when Sir Henry Bedingfeld and others were ordered by the Queen to exercise the garrisons in Norfolk, on account of the French, we read: "The Queen hath appointed Edmund Bedingfeld Esq, to bring of his own tenants 446 able soldiers, 45 at least to be skilful gunners and good archers."

Sir Edmund's daughters were, Elizabeth, who married Sir John Sulyard, Knight, and Margaret, who married, first Thomas Garneys, and second Bryan Rookwood in 1554.

Sir Edmund had charge of the unhappy Queen Catherine of Arragon, and attended her at the time of her death. The following letter from Henry VIII. is at Oxburgh, and addressed to Lady Bedingfeld, containing all instructions for the Queen's funeral. The hypocritical tone of the letter is apparent, and it is noticeable that he refers to his wife as "our dear sister."

THE BEDINGFELD CHAPEL, EXTERIOR VIEW.

" To our right trusty and well beloved,
the Lady Bedingfeld.
Henry Rex.

Right dear and well beloved, we greet you well: forasmuch as it has pleased Allmighty God to call unto His mercy, out of this transitory life, the right excellent Princess our dear sister, the Lady Catherine, relict, widow, and dowager of the right excellent Prince, our dear and natural brother Prince Arthur, of famous memory, deceased; and that we intend to have her body interred according to her honour and estate; at the interment whereof and for other ceremonies, to be done at her funeral and in the conveyance of the corps from Kimbolton, where it now remains, to Peterborough, where the same shall be buried, it is required to have the presence of a good number of ladies of honour. You shall understand we have appointed you to be there one of the principal mourners, and therefore desire and pray you to put yourself in a readiness to be in any wise at Kimbolton aforesaid the 25th day of this month, and so to attend upon the said corps till the same shall be buried and the ceremonies to be thereat done be finished. Setting you further to wite that for the mourning apparel of your own person we send you by this bearer — yards of black cloth; for the gentlewomen to wait upon you — yards; for two gentlemen — yards; for eight yeomen — yards; all of which apparel ye must cause in the meantime to be made as shall appertain: and as concerning the habiliment of linen for your head and face, we shall, before the day before limited, send the same unto you accordingly.

"Given under our signet at our manor of Greenwich the 10th day of January.

"And as forasmuch as since the writing hereof it was thought ye should be enforced to send to London, for the making of the said apparel for the more expedition, we thought convenient to desire you immediately upon the receipt hereof, to send your servant to our trusty and wellbeloved Councillor Sir William Paulet Knt, Comptroller of our household, living at the Friars Augustine in London, aforesaid, to whom bringing this letter with him for a certain token that he cometh from you, the said cloth and certain linen for your head shall be delivered accordingly."

Sir Edmund had been appointed Steward in Queen Catherine's household, and apparently he was under strict orders to report everything to the Privy Council. There is a letter extant from him giving details of a conversation he had with the Queen about her household. She desired him to retain "her confessor, her physician, and her potecary, two men servants, and as many women as it should please the King's grace to appoint, and that they should take no oath, but only to the King and her, *but to none other women*." The nature of the oath extorting obedience to the King and his "entirely beloved, lawful wife Queen Anne," explains this proviso.

Queen Catherine was then removed to Kimbolton Castle, where she commenced the dreary New Year of 1535. She was so badly off, that Sir Edmund wrote more than once that the household was quite devoid of money. The Queen was on her death bed before the end of the year, and the King received the first news of it from the Spanish Ambassador. Cromwell wrote instantly to Sir Edmund rating him, because foreigners "heard intelligence from the King's own castles sooner than he himself." Sir Edmund excused himself on the plea that his fidelity to the King's orders did not ingratiate him with the "lady dowager," who concealed everything from him. But he sent for the Queen's Spanish doctor, and questioned him about her Majesty's health. "I am informed," wrote Sir Edmund, "by her said doctor, that he had moved her to take some more counsel of physic, but her reply was: 'I will in no wise have any other physician, but wholly commit myself to the pleasure of God.'"

Lady Willoughby, the Queen's great friend, arrived at Kimbolton, cold and exhausted after a trying journey. At first Sir Edmund was not disposed to admit her to the Queen's presence, fearing lest she had not received permission from the tyrannical King to come. However he at length relented, and allowed her to approach the dying Queen, and she remained with her until the end.

The Spanish Ambassador also arrived, and was admitted to the Queen's presence. Sir Edmund reported that they conversed in Spanish, and therefore he could give no account of what passed. Sir Edmund next announced the death of the Queen, in these words: "January the 7th, about 10 o'clock. The lady dowager was aneled with the holy ointment, Master Chamberlayne and I being called to the same, and before 2 in the afternoon she departed to God. I beseech you that the King be advertised of the same." He added the following postscript to Cromwell:

"Sir, the groom of the chambers here can sere her, who shall do that feat, and further I shall send for a plumber to close her body in lead, the which must needs shortly be done, for that may not tarry. Sir I have no money, so I beseech your aid with all speed. Written at Kimbolton about 3 o'clock afternoon."

Sir Edmund and Lady Bedingfeld (the latter also having been with the Queen when she died) accompanied the coffin on the last sad journey between Kimbolton and Peterborough Abbey, on the 26th January. The funeral approached Peterborough by an ancient way from Kimbolton called Bygrame's lane. The last Abbot of Peterborough, John Chambers, performed her obsequies. "It was said that the day before Anne Boleyn was beheaded, the tapers that stood about Queen Catherine's sepulchre kindled of themselves, and after Matins were done, to *Deo Gratias*, the said tapers quenched themselves." The chamber hung with tapestry, in which Catherine of Arragon expired, is to this day shown at Kimbolton Castle. Miss Strickland, in her Life of the Queen, seems to imply that Sir Edmund was a "stern castellan," but reading between the lines I do not think so. It was his duty to carry out the task laid upon him, distasteful in many ways as it must have been. Perhaps he had the consolation of knowing that the suffering Queen trusted him; in happier days he and his wife had often been at Court, and were no strangers to her. From the fact that Mary Tudor, on coming to the throne, honoured Sir Edmund's son and successor with every favour and distinction, it is unlikely that the parents of her favourite courtier should have forfeited the esteem of Mary's beloved mother. Sir Edmund died and was buried at Oxburgh in 1554. The following particulars are taken from his will.[1]

"In the chamber called the King's Chamber a feather bed with a bolster, a mattress, a fustian covering of red and green sarsnet, a tester of black satin embroidered with unicorns and scallop shells. So many cushions with arms. A cupboard, with a green cloth thereon. Two chairs and a carpet in the window. Two irons in the chimney. Item—in next chamber a feather bed, bolster, pair of blankets, covering of tapestry, the hangings in the chamber of red and yellow. Item—in the inward chamber next into the chamber called the Queen's chamber a feather bed, with a bolster, a blanket ... a covering of russet cloth, a tester of stained cloth and a form, curtains of white linen cloth. In the Queen's chamber, a cupboard with a cloth thereon, 3 cushions without arms. Item in the chappell[2] a pair of chalices with the patent, the altar cloths, hangings, pale (pall) of whight sarsnet, 5 cushions, item, a cloth of black velvet with a whight cross, and I give to the said Sir Henry, one piece of silver, parcell gilt, where in is engraven God's blessing and the Bedingfeld arms, to remain to him as an heyre loom, in such wise as I received the same peice of my said brother Sir Thomas Bedingfeld."

[1] Deciphered from a document at Oxburgh by Sybil Lady Bedingfeld, 1909.

[2] This was probably a private chapel in the Hall or the mortuary chapel attached to Oxburgh Church.

Sir Edmund was succeeded by his eldest son Henry, who received the honour of knighthood, and married Katherine, daughter of John Townsend, Knight. These were troublous times for Catholics; the Book of Common Prayer had been drawn up, and it was enacted that places of public worship belonging to Catholics should be closed.

Many outbreaks took place on the part of the Catholics, who demanded the restitution of their religion; the people of Norfolk and Suffolk raised a rebellion under Kett. At length the Privy Council determined to send an army to suppress the outbreak, and the command was given to the Marquis of Northampton with many gallant knights, among whom is named Sir Henry Bedingfeld, and the King's troops occupied Norwich. To Sir Thomas Paston, Sir Henry Bedingfeld, and others, "men of approved valour and wisdom," divers parts of the city were entrusted, but the rebels came on them in the night, and a desperate fight ensued. Sir Henry Bedingfeld was taken prisoner and others, and a state of anarchy prevailed for three weeks afterwards. At length, after much fighting, the rebellion was quashed, and Kett hung at Norwich Castle, when we hope Sir Henry was released. The sweating sickness broke out in 1551, and at Norwich 960 persons died within a few days. The King, Edward VI., died in 1553, and the Council attempted to arrest the Princess Mary, but she took horse and rode in all speed to Norwich, partly that she might make her escape by sea if needful. "The fugitive heiress of England bent her flight in the direction of Cambridgeshire . . . and as the soft shades of a July night fell round her hasty course over those desolate plains ... once so familiar to the pilgrims going to Walsingham, the ladies and cavaliers discussed the recent death of the young King... They were all Catholics."[1] Wearied and worn, they arrived at Sawston Hall, and by the hospitality of Mr. Huddlestone, gladly given, they spent the night there.... A mob from Cambridge set fire to the hall next day. Queen Mary looked back from the Gogmagog Hills. "Let it blaze," she cried, "I will build Huddlestone a better," and she kept her word. By noon they reached Bury and pushed on to Norfolk. Among the earliest arrivals at Kenninghall to support the Princess were Sir Henry Bedingfeld, Sir Henry Jerningham, and Sir John Shelton. Sir Henry brought with him 140 men completely armed, and Mary removed to Framlingham Castle, a moated residence, while Sir Henry Jerningham proceeded to Yarmouth to rally the Queen's friends there. At Framlingham the Royal standard was hoisted, and a document at Oxburgh gives the details of the Duke of Northumberland's proclamation of Queen Mary at Cambridge. Another Oxburgh paper gives a letter to Sir Henry Bedingfeld from his son-in-law, Thomas Karrill, at St. Mary's, Wiggenhall, 13th July, 1553, showing that the Queen's cause was popular at Lynn and in the neighbourhood. In a note to this letter it is said that Mr. Karrill subscribed £26 13s. 4d. to the Queen's cause. Mary being such a good Catholic, it was reasonably hoped that the ancient religion would now be restored, and for Catholics her accession was an occasion of rejoicing.

[1] *Lives of the Queens of England.* Strickland.

The deprived Bishops were restored to their sees, Bishop Gardiner came back to Winchester and Bishop Bonner to London, and Mass was again said in all the churches.

The Bedingfelds were first and foremost in helping on the good cause. How fervently they and their co-religionists must have prayed for the Queen's happy marriage and an heir to the throne. In a letter to Sir Henry from one of the Privy Council is an interesting allusion to Philip of Spain, and his approaching visit to England.

" To the right honourable his verie loving friende Sir Henry Bedingfeld Knt. one of the Queen's most honourable privie Counsellors.

"After my most heartie commendations, you shall understand that yesterday the Queen's Majesty received advertisement from the Earl of Bedford, of his arrival in Spain, together with his great entertainment there, declaring that the Prince mindeth to embark the latter end of this month, and so to make so much haste hitherward as wind and water may serve. Other news worthy the writing here be none, but that all your friends here be well and merry, and glad to hear the semblable of you. Thus wishing unto you as unto myself, I bid you right heartily farewell, from the Court, the 26th March 1554.
" Your assured lovinge frende,
" EDWARD HASTINGS."

The Queen's marriage to Philip of Spain took place in 1554, on the 25th July, and England was reconciled

SIR HENRY BEDINGFELD, GOVERNOR OF THE TOWER.

to the Holy See, at the coming of the Papal Legate, Cardinal Pole, on the 30th November of this same year. After her coronation Mary appointed Sir Henry, Knight Marshal of her army, Captain of the Guards, Governor of the Tower of London, one of her Privy Council, and Vice-Chamberlain, with a pension for life of £100 a year, and part of the estate of Sir Thomas Wyatt, forfeited on his rebellion. A plot having been formed to execute the Princess Elizabeth, who was a prisoner in the Tower, the Queen became much displeased and alarmed, and sent for Sir Henry, with a hundred men of her Guard, to take command of the Tower, until she could form some plan to remove her sister from thence. The following letter relates to the Princess and her arrival at the Tower.

"To the right worshipfull Sir Henry Bedingfeld Knt.
give these
"Written in haste.

" My dutye remembered these shal be to advyse you that on friday my lady Elisabeth was sent to the tower at 10 of the cloke, the Parliament shal be holden at Westminster the daye afore assured and the Quene is in good helthe, thanks be to God, who preserve you in much worshipe thys good fryday, rydyng by the way,
" by yours to commande
"THOMAS WALTERS."

Sir Henry is described by his historians as a stern Norfolk knight, " in whose courage and probity " the Queen knew she could confide. The Princess was for some time in his custody, and in after years, when

Queen, used to playfully call him her gaoler. However, when she first saw Sir Henry, and the hundred men-at-arms, with their blue coats, under his command, enter the inner court of the Tower, she asked in terror "if the Lady Jane's scaffold was removed." The Lieutenant of the Tower endeavoured to calm her by saying there was no cause for alarm, but his orders were to consign her into the charge of Sir Henry Bedingfeld, to be conveyed to Woodstock. " Elizabeth, not knowing what manner of man Bedingfeld was, inquired whether he made conscience of murder, if such an order were entrusted to him."

The 19th of May she was removed from the Tower, first by barge at the Tower Wharf, and so to Richmond, where she had an interview with the Queen. The next day she crossed the river at Richmond, to proceed on her journey to Woodstock. The letters and State documents relating to this journey throw further light upon it. Sir Henry's note on the affair was as follows: "A memoriall off all letters, warrants, etc., whyche I have to shewe concerning the s'vice aboute my lady Elizabeth's grace, whereunto I was commanded by the Quene's highnes, which s'vice began the 8th off May 1554—and In the fyrst yere off hyr moste noble reign."

Anthony, Humphrey, and Edmund, brothers of Sir Henry, appear to have formed part of the guard brought by him to the Tower. In Sir Henry's report to the Queen of the journey from the Tower of London to Woodstock, he noted that the people between London and Windsor were not "hoole on matters of Religion" ... that "theye be fullye fyxed to stonde to the late abolyshyng off the byshopp off Romez aucthorite, as heretofore agaynste the order of all charite hath been establyshed by statute lawe within thys Realme."

The letter goes on to say that "My Ladye Elisabeth's grace" had not "been verye well at ease," and yet she wanted to go out walking. "In the whyche and other lyke hyr requests I am mervolouslye pplexed to graunte hyr desyer or to saye naye."

Then came "a remembrance off the journeye made by my Ladye Elizabeth's grace from Wyndsore to Syr Wyllm Dormer's house at West Wyckhm the xxth off maye 1 marie regine. Ffyrst when hyr grace cam to the castell gate to take hyr lytter, there stoode off Master Norrey's svnts xvj, in tawneye coots, to receyve hyr oute, at whyche place there weere sum people to behold hyr.... Itm, hyr grace passed the towne off Wyndsore wth moche gasyng off people unto Eton Colledge, where was used the like, as well by the scollers as others; the lyke in villages and ffeldes unto Wycombe, where most gasyng was used, and the wyves had p.pared cake and wafers wch at hir passing bye them, thei delyvered into the lytter. She receyved yt wth thanks untyll by the quantitee she was accombred and wth the herbes delyvered in with the wafers trobled as she sayde, and desyred the people to cease."

At West Wycombe, Sir William Dormer and 17 servants in "blewe coats" awaited her, half-a-mile from his house, with Lady Dormer and her daughter-in-law. At Woburn Sir Henry began talking with a "husbande man," and found him "a verye protestunte," and thought there were many about there of "the same opinion."

From the Dormers' house the Princess and suite went on to Lord Williams and thence to Woodstock. When the party arrived at this place Queen Mary sent instructions to "her trustie and ryght well beloved counsellor Sir Henry Bedingfeld knyght." She had reason to believe that Elizabeth was implicated in some conspiracy against her, and she wrote that in the face of so much evidence it was difficult to believe that her sister was guiltless of the charges brought. Sir Henry was admonished to continue his "accustomed diligence in the charge by us comitted to yow."

Then followed a report that "my ladye Elizabeth's grace ys daylye vexed with the swellyng in the face and other parts off hir bodye," and Sir Henry deputed Edmund his brother to declare the same to "my lorde Chamberlayne" and to ask for a doctor. "Doctour Owen" wrote directions to Sir Henry on the subject, and apparently thought it was not the "tyme off the yere to minster purgacions owing to the distemperaunce of the weather."

Then came a long letter to the Council relating various conversations between Sir Henry and the Princess, to which is added the following, "My lords it hath come to my knowledge by dyvse creditable and wrshipfull psons, that the remayneng off Cranmer, Rydleye, and Latimer, at Oxforde, in such sort as theye dooe, hath done nooe smal hurte In theys parts, even amonge thoose that were knowne to be goode afore."

The Queen's next letter to him affords proof of her thoughtfulness for others.

" The Queene's letter unto me."

" Mary ye Quene. By ye Quene.

" Trustye and right well beloved, we gret you well, and wheare we understande yt by occasion of certyn our instructions Latelye gyvene unto you, ye doe continuallye make your personall abode within that our howse of Woodstock without removing from thence, at anye time, which thing might p'adventure in continuance be both som daunger to your helth, and be occasion also yt ye shall not be so well able to understande the state of the countreye theare abowts, as other wyse ye might. We let you wit yt, in consideracon thereof we are pleased ye maye at anye tyme when yourself shall thinke convenyant, make your repayre from owt of our sayed howse, leaving one of your brethren to loke to yor charge, and se to the good goverunce of that howse in yor absence. So as nevertheless ye returne back ageyne yor self at night, for the batter loking to yor sayed charge. And for yor better ease and recreacon we are in lyke manner pleased yt ye and yor brethren maye at yor libertyes halk for yor pastyme at the partrige, or hunt the hare, wthin that our maner of Woodstock or anye of our grounds adioynyng to the same, ffrom tyme to tyme, when ye shall thynke moste convenient ; and that also ye maye yf ye shall so thinke good, cause yor wwf to be sent for, and to remayne theare wth you as long as yor self shall thinke meete. Geven under or signet, at or castle of Fernham ye— Julye, ye seconde yere of or Reigne."

Soon after Sir Henry wrote that if " this great

Ladye shall remayne in this howse, there must be repacons done bothe to the covering of the house in lead and slate, and especially in glass and casemonds, or elles neyther she nor anye yt attendethe uppon hir shal be able to abyde for coulde."

At length Sir Henry wrote to the Bishop of Ely, asking to be released from his post, as he had been for 15 weeks "·in care off mynde and some travell of bodye." He asks the Bishop to remind the Lord Chancellor (Bishop Gardiner) how at the latter's earnest request he had accepted the said post, in a talk they had, " uppon the caulseye (causeway) betwexte the house off saynete Jamys and Charyng Crosse." He further mentions he had asked for his Lordship's house at the " black friers " in London, but heard it was disposed of, therefore he asks for the one at "holbourn," as he has no house " off refuge in London, butte the comon Inne, and woulde be gladde to gyve large monye to be avoyded off that inconvenience."

Later, he is pleased to report to the Council that the Lady Elizabeth, after "hir confession in Catholyke fourme dydde receyve the most comfortable Sacramente," and before receiving she declared to Sir Henry " that she had never plotted against the Queene."

The Council replied that the Queen took great pleasure in the news that the Lady Elizabeth " doth so well conforme hirself in the receyvyng off the most blessed Sacramente off the altar." In a letter to the Queen Sir Henry gives some information as to Elizabeth using the reformed prayer book, etc., and refers to Mary's recent marriage, concluding with a reference to the hope of an heir to the throne, which would be a joy to all true Englishmen, "that wee maye as holye Simeon dydde for the byrth of Chryste, prayse Godde for the same." There seemed some difficulty in getting Elizabeth to give up the reformed prayer book, and she mentioned in reply to Sir Henry's remonstrance that it had been used in "the king my father his dayes."

Sir Henry had his doubts about her orthodoxy, and also of that of the ladies with her, and recommended that some "lerned men" should "preche and talke with them in the matter of there religion." He again asked to be released from his unwelcome task at Woodstock, but no answer came. The Princess asked for and obtained through Sir Henry's intervention a doctor and surgeon, and was bled in the arm and foot. She also requested to be moved nearer London, as there was great difficulty in conveying provisions to Woodstock during the winter.

At length came a letter from the Queen ordering Sir Henry to bring Elizabeth with all speed to Hampton Court, and the good "gaoler" was free to return home.

The following letter was evidently written to Sir Henry by his son-in-law, Henry Sackforde (or Seckford) before Sir Henry arrived at the Tower to take charge of the Princess. It is in the Oxburgh collection.

"To the right worshipful and his verie good master, Sir Henry Bedingfeld.

"My dutye always remembered, this maye be to

certifye unto you, that I have hired a stable at Charing Cross, and layed provision accordyng to your commandment. The stable will not hold above 6 Geldyngs, but I have covenanted with them to make·room at any time for three or four Geldyngs more, if need be. Sir if it might stande with your pleasure, I do think 6 Geldyngs nagges would serve your turn to attend upon the Queen's highness. Your chamber is prepared for you at My Lady Grayes who at this present doth attend upon my lady Elizabeth in the Tower. Your Pike's heads be covered over, and I have caused them to be stayed till your comynge uppe. Me Cosenes is your speciall good friend as apeareth in all his doynges towards you. Thus my dutie done, I leave you to Our Lord, who preserve you to the ende, From London the 22 of Marche.

"Your servante,
"HENRY SACKFORDE."

The following two letters relate to the time of Sir Henry's governorship of the Tower.

" Sir Henry Jernegan to Sir Henry Bedingfeld.
"To the right Worshipful Sir H. Bedingfeld Knt. After my most hearty commendations I have sent you this bearer to give attendance in John Leeke's place, who I have no doubt but that you shall find as quiet a man as you wole require, and further the Quene's Highness hath wylled me to certifye you that she hath lycenced Mr Cornwallis wife to resort to her Husband. I do and will labor all I can to have your company into Norfolk thys Lent, to course the Hare, and

Hawke the Heron, and thus I comyt you to God, praying hym to send us our Prosperity.

"Written at the Court the 16 day of Febr. 1556.
"Your assured HENRY JERNINGHAM."

Edward Lewkner, the subject of the following letter, had been groom porter to Edward VI. and Mary, and was condemned to death for partaking in the Dudley conspiracy. He fell very ill in the Tower, and Sir Henry interceded with the Queen on his behalf: his letter describing his (Lewkner's) death is at Oxburgh, with the following notes.

"The minutes of a letter to the Council 1556, when Edward Lewkner died, by Sir Henry Bedingfeld, by which he does not seem the hard hearted man some have supposed him, because he had charge of Queen Elizabeth when a prisoner." (In Charlotte Lady Bedingfeld's hand.)

"To the right honourable and mine especial good Lords of the Quene's Majesty's most honourable Privy Council.

"Please it your Grace and my Lords, to be advertised that this present Sunday, the 6th of Sept, Edward Lewkner, prisoner attainted, is by long sickness, departed this transitory Life to God about the hour of eight of the clock of the night. Who was a willing man in the forenoon of this day to have recd. the most Blessed Sacrament, but the Priest that did serve in the absence of the curate did think him so weak as it was not to be ministered to him, but after he had heard his Confession, he did minister unto him the Sacrament of Enelling or extreme unction, at the which I was present. Tomorrow I intend by God's grace to see him buried in form appertaining to his condition in law, as whereas I did learn of those that did see the like order. Instead of Will, he charged me, with his service to the Queen's Majesty, that it might please her highness after forgiveness of his offences towards the same, to vouchsafe to have pitty of his wife and ten poor children: which I promised to do at my next waiting upon her Majesty humbly beseeching your Lordships in the meantime to be Good Lords to the same his petition, and so as your poor beadsman do take my leave of you, from the Queen's Majestie's tower of London, 1556, the night abovesaid about 11 of the clocke. HENRY BEDINGFELD."

(The following note on this paper was made by Charlotte Lady Bedingfeld:

"Extreme unction, anointing with oil, a sacrament in the Catholic Church administered to those in danger of death—taken from St. James: 'If anyone is sick among you, let him call in the priests of the church, let them pray over him, anointing him with oil,' etc. etc.")

Good Sir Henry, this letter bears evidence of the solemn impression of a death-bed scene under which he wrote it. One feels sure the poor widow and ten children henceforth possessed a friend in him. "Tomorrow by God's grace I intend to see him buried." We can picture the incident for ourselves. A bell tolls slowly within the Tower precincts, and presently a coffin is carried out, the few bystanders kneel or cross themselves devoutly. The stately figure of Sir Henry is seen following, beads in hand, while he prays for the soul of his poor prisoner, whose earthly prison will know him no more.

That Sir Henry had interceded previously for Edward Lewkner can be seen by a letter received from one Francis Malet, a priest.

" To the right Worshipful Sir Henry Bedingfeld Knt Lieutenant of the Queens Highness's Tower of London give these.

"Right worshipful. After my hearty commendations these shall be to certify your mastership that where your Charity was declared in that it pleased you to take payns to declare by your wise and discreet letters the piteous state of Lewkner your prisoner, I was thereby the more ready . . . to move the Queen's goodness in the matter, And her grace being content to take into her hands your letter and having . . . withdrew into her privy chamber, sayd she would consider the matter and that I should know her pleasure therein afterwards, but as yet I cannot learn what her grace's resolute mind will be therein, and therefore to tarry this messenger any longer at this time I thought but folly, for that I shalbe ready sooner at night if it please her Highness to understand what answer she will make to my suit, or if it will not be known this night, as I doubt, for her grace is as it were defatigate with her late business in despatching the King of Bohemia's ambassador, I shall learn as soon as I may, what her grace's determination shalbe and that known I shall with expedition intimate the same unto you,

that so the poor man may be certified of the Queen's pleasure, And in the meantime I shall most heartily beseech your mastership to continue your favour towards the man, and divers of those that be most nigh unto her grace's presence, desire the same at your hands, and saith plainly that the Queen's grace will not be discontent that he have all the commodity that may be shewed him for the recovery of his health within the tower. I pray God show his Will mercifully upon him and I trust the Queen's goodness shalbe extended withall unto him to his great comforte, as knoweth Allmighty Jesus, Who send you with much Worship: long to live and well to like in both Soul and bodie. Scribled in haste with the running hande of
 " Yours to command
  " FRANCIS MALET, Priest."

The following paper from the Oxburgh Collections belongs to this time, and will be of interest:

"Instructions given by the King and Queens Ma^{jties} to their trustie and well beloved the Sheriffs and Justices of the Peace in the Countie of Norfolk, for the keeping watching and firing of the Beacons and the division and ordering of the people necessary to the same 3rd May 1557.

" (1) Our pleasure and commandment is our said Sheriffs and Justices of the Peace shall immediately upon the receipt of these their instructions assemble themselves together with as much speed as they possibly may in such place as they shall think most convenient, and at their meeting take such return, order, and direction of all the Beacons, as well on the sea coasts as others within land within the said Countie, and put in all readiness the places accustomed with all diligence.

"(2) Item, that the same Beacons be all from tyme to tyme diligently watched until ye shall receive order from us, or our Privy Council attendant upon our M^{aj}^{ties} to the contrery.

"(3) Item. Ye shall give special charge that in every permit appointed for the watching of any one Beacon, there be every night two honest householders at the least, appointed to watch the same.

"(4) We will that no Beacon be fired notwithstanding any number of ships be seen upon the Seas near the Coast, unless it shall plainly appear the said ships to approach near and attempt forcibly to enter, land, or do any hostilitie or annoyance to our Realm or subjects; in which case, if the number of ships be such as to require the assembly of any great force, we will the Beacons then be fired, to give warning to the country adjoining from the Sea Coast, to the intent they may also fire their beacons for the better withstanding of their enemies in their attempt, but not otherwise or upon any occasion other shall the Beacons be fired within the Land.

"(5) Item—that upon no occasion or business to fire any Beacon within land, unless it should appear that the Beacons that are about to give warning from the sea board to be first on fire, in which case the Beacons within land are also to be fired to give general warning.

"(6) Item for the avoiding of confusion and disorder

at the firing of the Beacons, if they shall require to be fired, and that the people should not wander up and down amazed at the same, we will that you take such order beforehand, as at the firing of the Beacon, you our said Sheriffs and Justices of the Peace, together with other gentlemen, constables, and other Officers of every profession, be then ready to resist the enemy.

"(7) Item, for the better order and stay of the People to appoint some one or two of the honest and staid men in every Parish unto whom the rest may refer and be directed by for their providing as the case shall require.

"(8) Finally we will and our pleasure is that you our said Sheriffs and Justices of the Peace shall diligently take order, for the well doing and executing of the premises within our said County accordingly. And further by common consultation amongst yourselves to devise and agree upon some such good means as you shall think best to understand in most speediest sort from what place and upon what occasions the first fire was given, to the intent that you may the more certainly be in order to make resistance accordingly.

"SUFFOLK."

Sir Henry's children were as follows: (1) Edmund, (2) Thomas, who married Anne Bedingfeld, (3) John, who married Margaret, daughter of Thos. Sulisden, by whom he had Francis, who married Catherine, daughter of John Fortescue, by whom he had three sons and twelve daughters, eleven of whom were nuns, and the twelfth was wife of Sir Alexander Hamilton, son of the Earl of Abercorn.

John Bedingfeld was a zealous Catholic and harbourer of priests; on one occasion the priest-hunters captured one of their victims under his roof, for which he had to pay a heavy fine. He constantly maintained a priest in his house. His long life was crowned with a holy and happy death. He was heard to say on his death-bed: "*Ecce nos reliquimus omnia et secuti sumus Te. Quid ergo erit nobis?*" (4) Nicholas of Snatshall who married a Downes. One of this family of Downes was committed to Norwich Castle for "obstynat papistrie" soon after the accession of Queen Elizabeth; and the infamous Topclyffe mentioned in a letter to the Earl of Shrewsbury, amongst the prisoners, "one Bedingfeld," and two others not worth memory for "baddness of belyfye." (5) Henry, who married Mary, daughter of Daniel de Acton.

The daughters were (1) Alice, who married first Thomas Capravill or Kervill, of Wiggenhall St. Mary, Esq., by whom she had a son, Henry, who married Winifred, daughter of Sir Anthony Thorold, whose son, Sir Henry, married a daughter of F. Plowden, by whom he had two children, who died in infancy. She (Alice) married secondly Henry Sackford, gentleman of the Privy Chamber to Queen Elizabeth. (2) Amy, wife of Thos Wilbraham. (3) Eve, wife of W. Yaxley, Esq. (4) Ruth, wife of W. Norton. (5) Elizabeth, wife of Edward Riches, of Swarington.

John Bedingfeld's son Francis, of Redlingfield in Suffolk, was father of the eleven nuns aforesaid. They were as follows:

Catherine, Superior of the Carmelites at Antwerp.
Mary, a nun at Liège.

Margaret, Abbess of the Poor Clares at Gravelines.
Winefride, a nun in Bavaria.
Helena, Abbess of the Austin nuns at Bruges.
Grace, a nun at Louvain (Canoness Regular).
Frances, a nun at Rome.
Philippa, a Benedictine at Ghent.
Anne, a nun at Gravelines. Fifth Abbess of the Poor Clares (died 17th November, 1697).
Magdalena, a Carmelite.
Mary, Abbess of the Austin nuns at Bruges.

Helena was the eldest, born in 1603; she went to St. Omers at the age of eight to live with her grandmother Fortescue, who brought her up. In 1622 she was professed. Margaret, the second daughter, made her profession as Sister Margaret of St. Ignatius at the Poor Clares at Gravelines in 1624, aged 19. Her distinguishing marks of sanctity were peace, confidence in God, and an all-embracing charity. Anne, the tenth daughter, became a Poor Clare; she was born in 1623, received the habit when sixteen, was elected Abbess in 1667, and died in 1697, having been in religion 57 years. Her portrait represents her with a cross, on one arm of which a dove is perched. This is said to relate to a vision with which she was favoured. Philippa took the name of Thecla in religion. She was of a "rare interior temper," having a gracious, sweet, and most meek disposition, yet of great courage in suffering. Catherine, born in 1614, took the name of Lucy of St. Ignatius, and entered the monastery at Dusseldorf. She died January 6th, 1650. " Her cheerful countenance, so true a picture of the interior joy of her holy heart, was able to encourage the most fearful." Magdalen joined the Order of St. Teresa, and was born in 1621, and is thought to have been the ninth daughter. In honour of St. Joseph she gave every day food and drink to a poor old man. She was elected Prioress of the Discalced Carmelites at Newbury, and until her death in 1684 she remained at her post. As Mistress of Novices she became eminent in an age when saintly guides in religious life were by no means rare. Like her model, St. Teresa, she had a strong clear intellect, great power of sympathy, and capacity for understanding the minds of others. The founder of their house, Duke Philip, Count Palatine of the Rhine, often sought her advice. Forty-three years after her death her body was found to be entire. " Mother Bedingfeld's body from time to time sends forth a very fragrant smell, her coffin is like new, the habit whole, her linen as white as if fresh put on." At the suppression of the convent in 1804 this coffin was moved to the Cemetery of St. George, Newbury. Mary, Winefride, and Frances, joined the "Institute of Mary." Winefride was born in 1610. She was placed at the head of the Munich convent; being exceptionally talented and discerning, she managed to free the house from debt. She was said to be so holy that she died of the force of her love for God. Frances was born in 1616. In 1623 she joined Mary Ward in Rome, and was much given to prayer and mortification. In 1650 she came to England to found a convent, and took a house at Hammersmith. The landlord looked at her with some suspicion, she thought, because she was so poorly dressed, but he told her he would trust her, " as being a Bedingfeld," though she was a stranger to him, " for Corronel Bedingfeld's sake, her kinsman, who was so worthy and honourable a gentleman, and just dead out of the house." The oil painting of Mother Frances, at the Bar Convent, York, represents her with regular features and fair complexion of the Saxon type; handsome, with great dignity of aspect. She bought the house and garden at York on the site of the present convent on November 15th, 1686. She was several times imprisoned in Ousebridge Gaol on account of her faith, and on one occasion the convent was about to be destroyed by a mob of infuriated men, but it is supposed they were frustrated by a miraculous occurrence. In 1699 Mother Frances was recalled to Munich, being then in her 84th year, and she left the community at York under the guidance of her great niece, Mother Dorothy Paston Bedingfeld, who was third daughter of Francis Bedingfeld of Redlingfield, and Mary, daughter of William Paston of Appleton, his wife. Reverend Mother Dorothy died in 1724.

To resume our history, Queen Mary died on November 14th, 1558, and among the bequests of her will, which was witnessed by Sir Henry Bedingfeld, was £200 to Sir Henry Jernegan. She was buried in Henry VII.'s Chapel. Elizabeth was crowned on January 15th, 1559, and when at her first Court Sir Henry came to pay his duty, she pleasantly said to him, " Whenever I have a prisoner who requires to be safely and strictly kept, I shall send him to you."

The following letter from the Queen is in the Oxburgh collection. It was written two years after her accession.

"Letter from Queen Elizabeth to Sir Henry Bedingfeld Knt.

"Elizabeth R. By the Quene.

"Trustie and well beloved we grete you well Lyke as we doubte not but by the comon reporte of the world it appeareth what great demonstracions of hostilitie the frenche make towards this Realme, by transporting great powers into Scotland upon the pretense onlie of theyre doinge about the conqueste of the same. So we have thought mete upon more certentie known to Us of their purpose to have good regarde thereto in tyme. And beinge verie Jalous of our towne of Barwick the principal keye of all our Realme, we have determined to sende with spede succours bothe thitherwarde to our frontier as well horsemen as fotemen. And do also send our right trustie and entirelie beloved cosen the Duke of Norfolk to be our Lieutenant general of all the north from Trent forward, for which purpose we have addressed our letters to sundrie our nobilitie and gentlemen in lyke manner as we do this unto you, willing and requiring you as you tender and respect the honor of Us, and suretie of your countrie, to put in redyness with all spede possible, one hable man furnyshed with a good strong horse or gelding, and armed with a corselet and the same to send to Newcastle by such further order for the furniture as shall be appointed to you by our trustie and well beloved Sir Edward Wyndham Knt, and Sir Christopher Heydon Knt, by whom we have advertysed of our further pleasure in that behalfe, and at the arrivinge of the sayd horseman at Newcastle he shall not onlie receyve monie for his rote and conduite, but also beside his wage, shall be by the direction of our said Cosen of Norfolk so used and entreated as ye shall not nede to doubt of the safe returne of the same, if the casualitie of death it be not empeached. And herein we make such sure accompte of your forwardness as we thereupon have signified among others to our sayd Cosen this our appoyntment and commandment, so shall we make accompte of you in that behalf whereof we pray you faile not. Given under our signet at our palace of Westminster, the 22nd day of December in the seconde yere of our Reyne.

"To our trustie and well beloved Sir Henry Bedingfeld, Knt."

Elizabeth's first Parliament voted her supreme head of the Church in England, and the Reformation Doctrines were established. There has been a constant tradition that the Queen paid a visit to Sir Henry at Oxburgh, and was lodged in what is still known as the Queen's room, and certainly at the beginning of her reign the Bedingfelds seem to have been more mercifully dealt with, as regards the change of religion, than might have been expected, but this state of tranquillity did not last, and evil days were in store for them. There are two letters of 1578, which tell their own story. The first is from the Bishop of Norwich, and the second from the Council. The Bishop was one Edmund Freke, promoted to the see of Norwich from Rochester. He was afterwards translated to Worcester, and was a Protestant and time server, as this letter shows.

"To the right worshipful, my loving friend, Sir Henry Bedingfeld Knt, in Norfolk, these after our right hearty commendations. It hath pleased my Lords of her Majesty's moste honourable privie councell at the sute of Mr Sackford your son in law, to permit you to remayne in your owne house untill our Ladye daie next, the rather for that their Lordships have been informed that, by reason of some great infirmitie you are not of habilitie to travail, and also it is hoped that within the tyme limited as aforesaid, you maie conforme yourself in matters of religion, of which your said libertie granted by mye said Lordes by their Letters of the 10th of this instant of Jannuarie, I am to advertise you and therewith have thought it good as one tenderlie regardynge the health of your soule charitablie to admonish you eftsoones both of the peril whereunto you are Lyable and subject in the sight of God, and her Majesty, most heartilie wishinge you conformitie therein and praying you to have consideration thereof, and of the ceremonie in this case observed. For as you are favourably dealt with for a tyme, so if the same do worke no amendment in you, you are then to repaire unto My Lords of her Majestie's moste honourable privie Council farther to be conferred with and ordered, as knoweth the Lorde to whom I commend you. From the Courte this 15th of Januarie 1578.

"Your loving frende,
"EDMUND NORWICH."

This letter was written at the beginning of the year, and apparently some months were allowed to pass, in the hope that Sir Henry would take the Protestant Bishop's advice, and conform to the State religion. But these exhortations had no effect upon him, and he was kept more or less a prisoner at Oxburgh, until summoned before the Council at the end of the year, when he was too ill to undertake the journey. His life from this year onwards became a true *via dolorosa* of persecution and physical suffering.

"To our loving Frende Sir Henry Bedingfeld Knt.

"After our heartie commendations. Whereas we are given to understand that upon some letters heretofore written, you are on the way repairing hither, forasmuch as we are informed by your son in law Henry Seckford, that your sickness and infirmitie is such as without danger you may not travel; we are very well contented if you shall not like to repair up, that you return again to the place where you be committed, there to remain untill such tyme as furder order shall be taken with you. And so fare you well from Richmonde, the firste of December 1578.

"Your loving frendes,

"BURGHLEY, T. SUSSEX, E. LYNCOLN, H. CROFT, F. WALSINGHAM."

Sir Henry's faithful son-in-law, Henry Seckford, was still watching over his interests as in happier times, and so events proceeded until three years later, when he was called upon to bear a further heavy sorrow in the death of his much loved wife, who was buried at Oxburgh December 7th, 1581.

The last letter from the Council gives him permission to leave his house for a time, to visit the Seckfords.

" From the Lords of the Council.
" To our very loving friend Sir Henry Bedingfeld, Knt.
" We commend us unto you. Whereas about three years past when that you were sent for to have appeared before Us, touching your disobedience in matters of religion, we were then moved in consideration of your sickness and infirmitie at the humble suit of Henry Seckford, your sonne, you being then in the waie hitherwarde, to license you to return back unto your own house whither you were before committed there to remain until further orders should be taken with you. And whereas at this time your sonne hath made lyke humble sute unto Us, that you maie be suffered to remove from your said house to St. Mary's Wignolles in Marshland a house of your daughter Seckforde, there to remain for a season untill you maie pass over the grief and remembrance of the Ladye your wyfe latelie deceased.

" These are in that respect to give you license so to do, and therefor you may at your lyking remove thither, contynuing yourself in lyke degree of restrainte as you dyd in your owne house. And these shall be your warrant in that behalf. So farewell from the Court at Whitehall, the 18th December 1581.
Your loving frendes,
SUSSEX,
W. BURGHLEY, T. BROMLET, CH. HALTON, JARNEYS SCOT. (FRA WALSINGHAM)."

But Sir Henry did not pass over his grief so easily, and only survived his wife two years, worn out by fines and imprisonments, and saddened by the spread of the heretical doctrines we know he so much abhorred. He passed away in 1583, aged 74, and was buried at Oxburgh on the 24th August of that year, "faithful unto death," and the type of a true-hearted Englishman of old times.

There is an interesting portrait of Sir Henry in the north library at Oxburgh; he is dressed in black velvet and ruff, and a gold signet ring, engraved with the family crest, on his hand. The expression on his face is resolute and thoughtful, with a shade of melancholy: he may have been fifty-five or sixty at the time. It has been said that Queen Elizabeth granted him the Manor of Caldecot, but it appears, by an old terrier in the reign of Edward VI., that the Caldecot Manor was then in the hands of the family. In a letter from Lady Bedingfeld, his wife, are some curious memorandums of household expenses written by Sir Henry, by which it appears that he kept twenty men-servants in livery, besides those employed in husbandry.[1]

---

[1] The following letter at Oxburgh was written by Lady Bedingfeld:

"Letter from Lady Bedingfeld to the Lords of the Council praying leave for her husband to be with her during her confinement.

"My Lord,

"Being very neere ye time of my being brought a bed and Sir Henry Bedingfeld in ye country, who is very tender in giving any offence to ye government this is humbly to beg your Lordship will be pleased so far to confirme ye order as he may have leave to be with me till ye time of my approaching danger be over and I shall ever acknowledge it as a very great favour done to

"Ye lordship's most humble servant."

On the other side of this paper is a prescription. The paper seems to have been addressed to the Earl of Shrewsbury, and was probably a

TOMB OF SIR HENRY BEDINGFELD, GOVERNOR OF THE TOWER, AND KATHERINE, HIS WIFE.

Sir Henry was succeeded by his eldest son Edmund, who was twice married, first to Anne, daughter of Sir Robert Southwell, of Hoxne in Suffolk, Knight, by whom he had issue, (1) Thomas, (2) Edmund, (3) Anthony, (4) Anne, wife of Robert Skerne, (5) Mary, wife of Sir William Cobb, Knight, and, (6) Nazareth, wife of Edward Yelverton; and secondly to Anne, daughter of John Moulton, of Thugarton in Norfolk, Esq., by whom he had no issue. Lady Cobb's husband owned Sandringham, and the following account is taken from a book about Sandringham which throws some light on Bedingfeld history at this period.

"The owners of Sandringham at various times intermarried with some of the principal Norfolk families, amongst others the Bedingfelds. . . . There stands not far from Swaffham one of the earliest and finest of the old houses of Norfolk, built in Henry the Seventh's reign by one of a family whose fortunes, character, and doings have invested Oxburgh with an historical

copy of the original letter. The writer had tried various ways of spelling Shrewsbury; the paper is not signed or dated. The following is the prescription:

"The lime Drinke against the King's Evill or any sharp Humours.

" Take unslackt Lime hott from the kill if you can gett it, and to every pound and half of Lime putt a gallon of water, if you putt 20 or 30 gallons of water to so many Pounds and halfe of Lime, it will not be worse for standing, some say it is the better, stirr the Lime well when all the water is in with a cleane stick, and when it bath stood 3 or 4 dayes, putt by the scum with a scimming dish, and take a gallon of the cleare water and putt it into an earthen pott, and putt into it of Liquorise aniseed Larcifar's(?) and currants of each a quarter of a pound. Beate your aniseed and currant a little and let it stand 48 hours. You may drinke halfe a pint in ye morning, halfe a pint at 4 o'clock in afternoone, and halfe when you go to bed, doe not take it from — for it will not drinke soe quick. Straine it when you take it out of the pott before you drinke it.

importance, as well as with the domestic interest which clings to walls within which generation after generation has lived and died. A hundred years after this stately house was built an unusually rapid series of deaths occurred in the Bedingfeld family. Sir Henry Bedingfeld, the 'Jaylor' of Queen Elizabeth, died in 1583, his son Edmund (of Ereswell in Suffolk, one of the Bedingfeld Manors) in 1585, and the son and heir of the latter, Thomas, in April, 1590. Thomas Bedingfeld had, among other sisters, Nazareth, who married Edward Yelverton, and Mary, who married Sir William Cobbe, of Sandringham. . . . The name of Mary Cobbe, Edmund Bedingfeld's daughter, is to be found in 1595 in the 'Popish Recusant' Rolls, those yearly lists, dating from the beginning of Elizabeth's reign, of the Catholics who refused to attend the worship of the Established Church, who denied the spiritual supremacy of the Crown, and who were in consequence subject to cruel penalties. . . . The houses of the ancient gentlemen's families in Norfolk who clung to the old faith were continually liable to be searched for suspected characters. Three or four miles from Sandringham, at Grimstone, lived Lady Cobbe's sister, Nazareth Yelverton, the virtuous and loving wife of Edward Yelverton, described, as well as her sister, as a 'recusant.' Edward Yelverton, whose name is in the list of Popish recusants in Norfolk and Suffolk, 1596, was the son of William Yelverton of Rougham, his family being very influential in Norfolk at that time. From an entry in Le Neve's *Norfolk Collections*, it appears that 'Edward yelverton the recusant' lived at Grimstone and Appleton. He also had a 'smale

CLEMENT PASTON.

house' at Wolferton. He was buried in Sandringham Church, after a life-long devotion to the Catholic cause, which cost him imprisonment and many other sacrifices. . . ."

At this time Sir Edward Paston was building a fine new house at Appleton. He acquired the land from his uncle, Clement Paston, of Caistor and Oxnead (the latter was a well-known commander in the reign of Mary and Elizabeth). "The Pastons liked building beautiful houses. Clement had, at the time of the building of Appleton House, just finished the magnificent family seat at Oxnead. Sir Edward Paston is said to have built Barningham Hall, in the east of Norfolk, in 1612, and also Thorpe Hall, near Norwich. The selection of Appleton for a mansion is thus accounted for. He had begun building at Binham, on the priory ground which Henry the Eighth had granted to his father, when an accident occurred which so shocked him that he relinquished his purpose. While clearing some of the ground a piece of the wall fell on a workman and killed him. Edward Paston's conscience smote him, and he would have no more to do with secularizing consecrated ground. He therefore built his house at Appleton, and lived there until he was past eighty, close to the gates of the Cobbes. . . .

"The date on the gate-house was 1596. Clement Paston died in 1597. The house was burnt in 1707, and is thus described by Le Neve: '1726. Appleton Hall burnt to the ground on the day of . . . 1707.' The Cobbes of Sandringham were friendly for more than a century with the Le Stranges of Hunstanton Hall. In 1520 'Mr. Cobbe and his wyff stayed at Hunstanton where they met the Prior of Coxford, etc. and had for dinner a crane, six plover and a brace of rabbits.' In 1533 'Mestrys Cobe and hyr syster with others of the countreye,' were guests at Hunstanton, and it was probably there that the Cobbes made the acquaintance of the Bedingfeld family, many of whom, especially 'Edmund Bedingfeld,' were constantly staying there."

Edmund Bedingfeld did not long survive his father, and died in 1585, aged 51, and was succeeded by his eldest son, Thomas Bedingfeld, who married Frances co-heiress of John Jerningham, of Somerley town in Suffolk, Esq., by whom he had two sons, viz., Henry and William. Thomas died in 1590, and was succeeded by his eldest son Henry, who was only nine years old at the time he was left fatherless. His mother, Frances Bedingfeld, married, secondly, her cousin, Sir Henry Jerningham, of Cossey, who appears to have managed his stepson Henry's property, the boy having a long minority.

The following paper at Oxburgh seems to show that the fine old property had fallen much out of repair, owing doubtless to the fines and imprisonments endured by its late owners, who had died in rapid succession. (The first part of the paper relates to the earlier period).

"A seize taken the 23rd of January in the 4th year of the reign of our sovereign lady Elizabeth, by the grace of God, of England, and Ireland, Queen defender of the faith by us, H. Branthole gent her Majesty's feodary, for the county of Norfolk etc, by virtue of

Her Highness' commission out of her Majesty's court of wardes, herewith annexed to us directed, of the house of Oxburgh in the county of Norfolk, being the chief mansion house of Henry Bedingfeld Esq. nowe her Majesty's warde, of all such decayed places there as doe neede present reparation of tymber work, and what number of okes trees are necessary for the same decayes, by view and advise of Robt Booke and W. Bandy carpenter, being called thereto by us the sayd Commissioners here present.

"*Imprimis.* for the repairing of the little mill house and chamber over the sayd house being 25 feet in breadth and 24 in length 32 okes."

(This mill used to stand where is now the "Millerslay Bank" in the Park at Oxburgh; some of the brickwork is still there to be seen (A.D. 1912). It was turned by the stream that feeds the moat, and runs through the sluice down by the drawbridge and into the park beyond).

"Item for planks and joices for the great stable, being in length 24, and in breadth for the horse standing 9 feet: 30 okes. Item to plancher the granary chamber over the same stable being 20 feet wyde and 24 feet long, with the help of the old planche, 5 okes.

" Whereas a commission was awarded out of His Majesty's Court of Wards . . . to you and others to survey and view the several decayes of the Manor House of Oxburgh in the countie of Norfolk with the Ediface's and buildings there to belonging, and the Manor house of Stratton lately consumed with fire, and what tymbers will serve as well for the repairing

of the sayd decayed house and buildings of Oxburgh ... of the possession of Henry Bedingfeld His Majesty's warde ... the same will require by the judgement of and opinion of sundry carpenters also viewing the sayed decayes, and the tymber trees growing in a wood called Norton(?) Woode, where the same may be most conveniently had 160 trees etc. .. These are therefore to will and require you to assigne and appoint unto Henry Jernegan Esqre, comittie of the saide warde his executors ... the nombre of 277 trees to be taken in the sayde woode called Norton Woode ... etc signed
"HENRY BRANTHWAYTE Esq.
"WM BURGHLEY.
"dated 14 February 1597."

Henry Bedingfeld was then aged sixteen, and his mother, Lady Jerningham, died the following year, 1598, having survived her first husband eight years. She gave birth to a son the year before she died, as may be seen by an entry in the Oxburgh parish register, as follows: "1597 baptised Ferdinando the son of Henry Jernegan Esq. and Frances his wife, 21st August in Oratorio Proprio." Sir Henry Jerningham (young Henry's stepfather) made his will two years before the death of his wife, in 1596. He gives to his wife Frances the wardship of her son Henry Bedingfeld, "also the lease of his lands which I hold of the Queen during the minority of the said Henry; also to her all my goods and all my household goods at Oxburgh which I bought of the executors of her late husband Thos Bedingfeld Esq.

SIR HENRY BEDINGFELD, WHO WAS IMPRISONED IN THE TOWER, FATHER OF FIRST BARONET.

also all his plate except such as is before disposed to my children; also all my horses, geldings, naggs, sheep, and other cattle, as also all my stuff and household furniture at Cossey and Wingfield."

Sir Henry died in 1619, and was buried in St. Margaret's Church, Westminster. In the history of Norfolk, mention is made of a visit to Oxburgh by the pursuivants in 1590 in the following terms :

"In consequence of information against Henry Bedingfeld of treasonable designs with Papists and Recusants diligent search is made at the house of Henry Bedingfeld, but nothing suspicious found."

Many other members of the family had suffered during these years for their Faith. In 1574 Anthony Bedingfeld is amongst the lists of convicted Papists, and Humphrey Bedingfeld several times prosecuted for hearing Mass. In 1580 Humphrey Bedingfeld was committed for Papistry. In 1585, amongst Papists refusing to come to church are Edmund Bedingfeld, Humphrey Bedingfeld of Quidenham, Henry Bedingfeld, Laurence Bedingfeld of Holme Hall, Elizabeth Bedingfeld (widow of Henry Bedingfeld), and all fined yearly.

Having lost his mother and stepfather, Henry Bedingfeld married his first wife about 1604, when he was twenty-three. His first wife was Mary, daughter of Lord William Howard, of Naworth Castle in Cumberland (third son of Thomas Duke of Norfolk), by whom he had a son Thomas, steward of the Duchy of Lancaster, who married Mary, daughter of Robert Brooksby, of Sheffield in Leicestershire, and died suddenly at Oxburgh April 26th, 1665, at the age of sixty, in consequence of wounds he had received in the head during the civil wars. Henry married a second time in 1611. His second wife was Elizabeth, daughter and co-heiress of Peter Hoghton, of Hoghton Towers in Lancashire, Esq., by whom he had four sons and four daughters, (1) Henry, (2) William, a captain in the Guards and a great favourite of the famous Duke of Lorraine, who married a widow and died without issue, (3) Edmund, eminent for his piety, and a Canon of Lierre in Brabant, where he died, (4) John, who died unmarried. The daughters were (1) Jane, married Colonel Apreece, of Huntingdonshire, (2) Elizabeth, married Thos. Timperley, of Hintlesham, in Suffolk, Esq., (3) Mary, married William Cobbe, of Sandringham, Esq., (4) Anne, married Richard Martin, of Motford, in Suffolk, Esq. Henry Bedingfeld's first wife, Elizabeth Howard, was, as already said, daughter to Lord William Howard, and her mother was Elizabeth, daughter of Thomas, Lord Dacres of Gillestail. Her grandfather was Thomas, fourth Duke of Norfolk, beheaded June 2nd, 1572, and her grandmother was Margaret, daughter to Lord Audley, widow of the Duke of Northumberland, and second wife to the Duke of Norfolk. Elizabeth Bedingfeld's eldest brother was ancestor to the Earls of Carlisle. Mary Brooksby, who married Thomas Bedingfeld, was daughter of Robert Brooksby, Esq., of Staunton and Shouldham, in Leicestershire. The family of Brooksby were lords of those places in the reign of Edward the Third. William Brooksby, father to Mary Bedingfeld, died in 1606. Mary having no issue, the property went to his other daughter, Winifred, who conveyed it into the

LADY BEDINGFELD (*née* DE HOGHTON), SECOND WIFE OF SIR HENRY BEDINGFELD, THE PRISONER IN THE TOWER.

Englefield family, by her marriage with Francis Englefield, Esq. Henry Bedingfeld was knighted during the Civil Wars, with his two eldest sons, Thomas and Henry. He flew to the Royal Standard at the very beginning of hostilities. Thomas was made a colonel, and Henry a captain of horse. Both exhibited great courage in defending the cause they had so loyally embraced. The period of the last seven years of Charles the First's reign was for them fraught with adventures and suffering. A second alliance had taken place between the families of Bedingfeld and Cobbe, Elizabeth, daughter of Sir Henry, having married Colonel William Cobbe.[1] The latter, Colonel Cobbe, suffered not only as an active Royalist, but also as a recusant and Papist. The sequestration of the estates of Catholic Royalists was one of the principal sources of revenue upon which the Commonwealth depended.

Sandringham, the Cobbe's property, in common with most other estates of Papists and delinquents, was sequestered in 1643, "about Michaelmas, just after the siege of Lynn," when it is likely Colonel Cobbe sent assistance to the garrison. That ever loyal town stood out bravely against the Duke of Manchester's forces, but was compelled to capitulate.

Sir Henry Bedingfeld, Sir Hamon Le Strange, his son Roger, and others, went to the defence of Lynn on horseback, "they and their men armed with swords and pistols." A curious old narrative of the siege of Lynn states that Sir Henry Bedingfeld was one of the

---

[1] This Mrs. Cobbe had several children, five daughters, Elizabeth, Dorothy, Anne, Mary, and Frances. The first four entered religion in convents abroad, where they died.

hostages kept until the conditions of the surrender had been fulfilled.

Sir Henry was taken prisoner and committed to the Tower in 1647, for upwards of two years, during which time Oxburgh was besieged by Cromwell and his Roundheads. They attempted to burn down the castle, and remains of the charred timber can be seen to this day (A.D. 1912) in the attics of the east wing. The fire was unaccountably checked before doing any damage. Sir Henry's estate, or a great part of it, was sold by the rebels, and the rest sequestered, during his life. During his imprisonment in the Tower he wrote a book, dated 1649, on the Passion of our Saviour, and dedicated it to his second wife in the following terms :

" My Deare,

"I that have loved your person so dearly, as I have done for this thirty eight years, and acknowledging the like return of your affection to me againe, I cannot be ungrateful to God, who hath bestowed so great a blessing on me as you yourself, to be unmindful of your spiritual comfort in these most miserable and distracted times, which doth amase the greatest spirits, that now liveth : and for my part I must confes my weeknes to be such, that if it had not bine for Medditating of this following treates, it would have shaken me much ; but cinse I have looked upon the goodness of God, and the sufferings of our Blessed Saviour, I am by His grase and goodness so comforted as I wish that if it were His holy Will, I might beare a greater part of His Blessed Cros then yet I have done, for I know my crimes hath deserved it, but to His heavenly will and pleasure I resine you and myself.

"From the Tower in London the 20th of February 1649."

In another leaf of the book, his second son Henry, first Baronet, wrote many years later.

"22nd November 1676.

"This booke was written with my dear Father Sir Henry Bedingfeld's own hand whilst he was a prisoner in the Tower, wheare he was one yeare and three quarters, procured his release about Hollimas 1649: his estate was sold over his head for delinquency in the year 52; he departed this life after many sufferings 22nd November 1659, haviug been ill of a quartan ague and the dropsy ten weeks; he lies buried in Oxburgh Church near the tomb of his predecessor aged 75 yeares and a half.

"HENRY BEDINGFELD, his second sonne, editis."

Sir Henry added the following note about his brother Thomas dying at Oxburgh. This Thomas had married Mary Brooksby of Leicester, who survived him.

"My elder brother Thomas died the 26th of April 1665, beinge Wednesday by two in ye morninge of an apoplexi, he came downe from London to cutt downe Timber and rayse money and it pleased God, he fell sicke, suddenly he died; the same day I engaged for £500 to redeem the timber, and keepe the houses from beinge pulled downe. He lived nine years after my father, and was 60 yeares old when he died."

Thomas was known as the "Colonel," and his widow, "Mrs. Marie Bedingfeld," survived him fourteen years, dying August 1st, 1679. She married a Mr. Harrison, and died at his house in Suffolk.

The following letter from Colonel Thomas Bedingfeld to his brother Henry Bedingfeld, is at Oxburgh:

"To my honored Brother Henry Bedingfeild [1] Esquire, Beckhall.

"My dearest Brother,

"I thank you for the favour in sending me a warrant for a —— which will be less chargeable than out of Norfolk and am glad to hear you spend your Christmas so merrily in the country. There is a rumour that the Duke of Norfolk shall be sent for over. I hope it will not prove true. My business with the New England people I believe is carried with so high a hand against me that the most I can get will be the arrears which is the very most of my hopes. I have taken advice about the enclosing of the common at Stoke. I am assured if I do not presently begin that work it will be much to my disadvantage the Commissioners sitting but thrice more when all things will be concluded their first meeting will be 17th of February the second in Easter week and their last in Whitsun week. I have been with Mr. Jonas Moore who hath undertaken that work for me I must choose four commissioners for me to treat with the tenants and set out my part whereof Mr Moore to be one yourself and Robert Hamond and Mr Win the rest I am glad to

[1] In all Thomas Bedingfeld's letters he invariably misspelt his name.

COLONEL THOMAS BEDINGFELD.

hear of the agreement between Mr. Cooke and Sir Nicholas Strange to satisfie Drewitt[1] that I am not the first nor the only person that begins to enclose. Sir Henry North is now beginning with Mildenhall and all Lords will do the like as fast as they can there was a —— to put off the meeting of the Parliament and dissolve but it would not pass there is nothing here of news only the indisposition of my Lord Chancellor with the gout I shall expect your pott of ducks which I had rather have than teal I give many thanks for them and remain your most affectionate brother and friend

"THO BEDINGFEILD

"London the 31st of December 1663."

The reference in the beginning of this letter to the "New England people" is to be explained by the fact that the properties of Elvedon and Cavenham belonging to the Bedingfelds, were taken from them for recusancy and given for the "Propagation of the Gospel" in New England.

Sir Henry Bedingfeld is generally known as "the prisoner in the Tower," and it is consoling to know that he obtained his release and was restored to his wife and family eight years before his death. Probably he never recovered entirely from the effects of his imprisonment, as he was then sixty-two years of age. His portrait in the east wing at Oxburgh represents him in armour, with long hair and moustache of the Cavalier Period. His wife's portrait is in the west wing passage. She is all in black, with black peaked

---

[1] Mr. Edward Drewett. (See page 67.)

cap, and white about the neck and sleeves, a shrewd kindly old face. There is a full-length picture of a lady in black in the saloon, formerly supposed to be Mary Queen of Scots, but the ruff being of a later period, it has been suggested that it was this Lady Bedingfeld (*neé* de Hoghton) in her youth.

Against the north wall of the chapel at Oxburgh is a lofty monument of black and white marble, ornamented with festoons, etc., below, two shields supported by two angels, on one of which is this inscription : " Under this monument lyeth the body of Sir Henry Bedingfeld, the 17th Knight of this family, eminent for his loyalty to his prince and service of his country. In the time of the rebellion he was kept three years prisoner in the Tower and great part of his estate was sold by the rebels, the rest sequestered during his life. He had two wives: the first Mary, daughter of William Lord Howard of the north, by whom he had one son, who died without issue. His second wife was Elizabeth, daughter of Peter Houghton Esq., by whom he had five sons and six daughters. He died November 22nd, 1657, aged 70 and six months."

On the other shield :

" Here lyeth Elizabeth, wife of Sir Henry Bedingfeld Knt. and daughter of Peter Hoghton of Hoghton Tower in Lancashire, Esq. She died on the 11th April Anno Domini 1662.

"'Beati mortui qui in Domino moriuntur.' Eccles."

Sir Henry's dates differ from those on the tomb as to his father's age at the time of his death : also as to the year of his death.

The following notes as to some Bedingfeld pro-

MONUMENT IN THE BEDINGFELD CHAPEL (ATTACHED TO THE PARISH CHURCH OF OXBURGH) TO SIR HENRY BEDINGFELD (THE PRISONER IN THE TOWER) AND HIS TWO WIVES, ALSO TO THE FIRST BARONET AND HIS WIFE (*née* PASTON).

perties are taken from a paper written by Margaret, Lady Paston Bedingfeld, and copied from Blomefield's *History of Norfolk.*

"*Hale Manor.* From the Jennys it came to the Bedingfelds, and in the reign of Elizabeth, Anthony Bedingfeld, Esq., 3rd son of Sir Henry Bedingfeld of Oxburgh, was Lord of Hale Manor, and married Elizabeth, one of the daughters and co-heirs of Ralph Danyel of Swaffham gent. Anthony Bedingfeld, of Testerton in Norfolk, descended from the aforesaid Anthony, died Lord in 1701, whose son Francis sold it to Henry Ibbot of Swaffham, attorney.

"*Bures Hall.* A capital messuage annexed to the other, and sold by the Bedingfelds to the Eyres. Several of the Bedingfelds were buried in Holm Hale Church, amongst others Mary, daughter of Sir Henry Bedingfeld, late of Beck Hall, Knight and Bart., and widow of Thomas Eyre of Bury's Hall, Esq. She was very exemplary and eminent for her charity, piety, and other virtues, died 28th September, 1710, aged 67.

"*Foulden.* Margaret, relict of Edmund Bedingfeld, Esq., sister and heiress to Sir Thomas Tuddenham, died seized of the Manor here (which descended to her from the Weylands and the Limeseys) in the 15th of Edward 4th.

"*Cley.* In the 33rd of Henry 8th Sir Edmund Bedingfeld, Henry Bedingfeld and Katharine his wife held this manor.

"*Necton* was granted by Queen Mary (2nd and 3rd of Philip and Mary), as is expressed in the patent, to her beloved and faithful counsellor Sir Henry Bedingfeld of Oxburgh, being parcel of the possession called Warwick Lands, with the wood called the Necton Wood and Park, the manor of Westacre in Grimston and Congham, the manor of Hillington, the Manor of Uphall alias Ashill, Collards and Games, with the advowson of the church of Ashill, in consideration of his surrendering a pension of £100 per annum granted him by the said Queen for life, for his services at Framlingham in the late rebellion, and also in exchange for the Manors of Wald, Hewton, and Baynton, in Yorkshire, granted as above, and it was continued in the family until it was sold to Henry Eyre, Esq., of Bures Hall in Hale.

"*Caldecot* was brought into the Bedingfeld family by Margaret Tuddenham, sister and heir of her brother, Sir Thomas Tuddenham.

"*North Pickenham*. On the division of the last Lord Latimer's estate, about the 20th of Queen Elizabeth, this manor was sold to the Bedingfelds of Oxburgh, and in the 32nd of the said Queen, Thomas Bedingfeld, Esq., sold a fald course, etc. In the family of Bedingfeld the manor with remaining demesnes continued till about the 12th of George 1st, when Sir Henry Bedingfeld, Bart., sold it to Henry Eyre, Esq., of Bures Hall in Hale.

"*Houghton on the Hill*. Soon after the death of the last Lord Latimer (temp Elizabeth) this lordship came into the family of the Bedingfelds of Oxburgh, and in this family it continued till it was sold by Sir Henry Bedingfeld about the year 1720.

END OF THE FIRST PART.

SIR HENRY BEDINGFELD, FIRST BARONET.

The Bedingfelds of Oxburgh.

PART II.
NOTES ON THE BARONETS OF THE FAMILY.

M.DC.LVII.—M.DCC.LX.

THE first Baronet of the family was Henry, second son of the illustrious "Prisoner in the Tower of London," and his second wife, Elizabeth, daughter of Peter de Houghton Esq. He survived all his brothers and sisters, and enjoyed a long tranquillity after the Restoration of Charles the Second, who made him a Baronet for the great and eminent services done by the Bedingfelds to the cause of the Stuarts. Unfortunately the King did not repay him the £45,000 which these "great and eminent services" had cost the family. Sir Henry allowed his patent to lie dormant for many years, which "postponed him to many in point of seniority." He was thought to be one of the most accomplished men of his time, "tall and comely, endowed with rare parts both natural and acquired." His life was most exemplary, and he was admired for his virtue and wisdom. He married Margaret, daughter and heiress of Edward Paston, of Horton, Gloucestershire, Esq., and Appleton, Norfolk, and had three sons

F

and five daughters, (1) Sir Henry, his successor, (2) John, who married Dorothy, daughter and co-heiress of John Ramsay, and had issue, (3) Edward,[1] married Mary, daughter of Sir Clement Fisher, of Packington, Warwickshire, Bart. The daughters were, (1) Elizabeth, wife of Thos. Whetenhall of East Peckham in Kent, Esq., (2) Frances, wife of Richard Caryll, of Harting, Sussex, Esq., (3) Mary, second wife of Thomas Eyre, of Hassop, Derbyshire, Esq., (4) Margaret, (5) Anne, both Carmelites at Lierre, in the Province of Brabant, where the former became Superior or Abbess. The Very Rev. Edmund Bedingfeld, brother of the first Baronet, was a Canon of Lierre, and confessor to the Carmelite nuns of that place. His portrait is at Oxburgh, but during his life he was an exile from his beloved home and country, "even from his youth," owing to his religion. It was written of him that he had a particular devotion to the Blessed Virgin, that though distinguished by his birth, he was much more so for his prudence, learning, and purity of life, which was so remarkable as to make him appear angelical to men and odious to the devils, which they publicly showed on several occasions. His disinterestedness was extraordinary, for although he served the community gratis and entirely at his own expense, for the space of thirty-two years, he could never be prevailed on to receive any small presents they were often out of gratitude solicitous to give him, "which makes them look upon this as one of the least acknowledgments they can make to so signal a benefactor, who was and

[1] Edward Bedingfeld's daughter Mary married Sir John Swinburne in 1721, and died in 1761. Her portrait is at Oxburgh.

MARY LADY SWINBURNE, DAUGHTER OF EDWARD BEDINGFELD OF YORK (YOUNGER SON OF FIRST BARONET). SHE WAS MARRIED TO SIR JOHN SWINBURNE IN 1721 AND DIED IN 1761.

EDMUND BEDINGFELD, CANON OF LIERRE.

is still esteemed to have been one of their principal helps in the beginning of this foundation." He wrote the life of a very holy nun at Lierre, Mother Margaret Mostyn, and relates that Sir Henry, his brother, was present at her death-bed in 1678. Mother Margaret thanked Sir Henry on that occasion for all he had done for their house, and promised to pray for him. There is a letter amongst the Oxburgh papers from the good Canon to Mr. Drewett (who evidently acted the part of agent at Oxburgh during this period).

"I.H.S.

" Worthy Sir,

"This weeke made me happy with one from you, accompagned with a bill . . . from my cousin Paston, for which I must retourne you many thanks, for though it came late, I had rather by farre have it soe, than by peece meale's as formerly. I hope all my friends about you are well, to whom I beseech you present my true service, and if I can at any time serve you, you shall find mee most ready, desiring to show myself in somewhat greatfull for soe many favours. Ever remayning your true friend, ED. BEDINGFIELD, Cannon at Lier. 9th of November, 1667. To my worthy friend Mr. Edward Drewett these. Norfolke at Oxborowe."

A younger brother of Sir Henry's was John, killed at the Battle of Worcester at the early age of sixteen. He was a captain of horse in the King's army, and his portrait in the saloon at Oxburgh represents him in armour, with flowing hair, a very handsome young officer.

Dame Margaret was married to Sir Henry at the early age of sixteen (he being twenty). Her mother was Frances, daughter of Sir John Sydenham, of Brymston in Somersetshire, who died Feb. 15th, 1665. Dame Margaret must have had much to suffer from the turbulence of the times in which she lived. Her husband, with his father and brother, joined the Royal Standard at the breaking out of the Civil War, and after bravely risking their lives in many desperate actions to support their Royal master, they shared in his misfortunes. Sir Henry escaped to the Continent with his brother, and Lady Bedingfeld remained in England, managing her husband's concerns with the utmost prudence. Her husband is said to have declared in his dying moments "that she had been a wife who had never once displeased him." Her eldest son wrote of her in his memorandum book, in the year 1699 or 1700, " My mother, aged neer 80, is in perfect health, and in all probability may live many yeares. She is still a woman of great witt and quick partes, but very partiall in her affections." Dame Margaret was buried in the chapel at Oxburgh. On her monument she is described as " a person of extraordinary parts, piety, and prudence, who after fifty years' enjoyment of perfect felicity in the married state, passed eighteen years' widowhood in an absolute retreat, in the constant exercise of her devotions, and daily distribution of charity, and departed this life January 14th, 1703, aged 84 years." Her portrait hangs on the north staircase at Oxburgh. She is in black velvet, the bodice trimmed with fichu and cuffs of rare lace, and fastened with a knot of pearls on black velvet. Dame

MARGARET PASTON LADY BEDINGFELD (ÆT. 18) WIFE OF FIRST BARONET.

WILLIAM PASTON, SECOND EARL OF YARMOUTH
(*From a portrait at Oxburgh.*)

Margaret appears again in the votive picture of her husband and herself, kneeling beneath the mantle of the Blessed Virgin, surrounded by their children. She has left another memento of herself at Oxburgh in the quaint heraldic vane on the top of the venerable tower, as firmly fixed now as when first placed there by her directions. Father Pollen, in the *Catholic Records*, gives a letter from Margaret Lady Bedingfeld to the Dowager Lady Yarmouth (the original manuscript is in the British Museum). The date of the letter is conjectured to be about 1683, and it relates to Lord Yarmouth's visit to Norfolk soon after his accession to the Earldom. He had married a natural daughter of Charles the Second, the Lady Charlotte Fitzroy. The following account of the Paston family at this date is given in a paper which has lately come into the possession of Sir Henry Paston Bedingfeld, together with a small engraved portrait of Lady Paston.

"Sir Robert Paston of Paston in ye county of Norfolk, was for his great service in ye Late Troubles and Activeness for ye King's Restoration, by letters Patent bearing date at Westminster 25 Car II, advanced to ye Degree of a Baron of this Realm by ye Title of Lord Paston of Paston in ye same county of Norfolk; as also The Dignity of a Viscount, by ye Title of Viscount Yarmouth, and to ye Heirs Male of his Body. He married Rebecca, the second Daughter of Sir Jasper Clayton, Knight Citizen of London, by whom he hath had Issue, six sons, and four Daughters. His eldest son William hath taken to wife The Lady Carlotte Fitzroy, one of the Natural Daughters of King Charles the Second."

There is also at Oxburgh a prayer-book of the Elizabethan period, formerly belonging to Dame Margaret, and to her mother, and grandmother before her. It is called the Sydenham Prayer-Book. Dame Margaret's mother was a Sydenham, and thus the book came to the Bedingfelds. It contains, amongst other items of interest, a prayer of Queen Mary Tudor, entitled " Good Queen Mary's prayer, which she used everye mornyng all her lyfe tyme."

Some other interesting papers amongst the Oxburgh collection relate to Dame Margaret's uncle, Wolstan Paston, who was the son of Edward Paston, by Margaret his wife, daughter of Sir Thomas Berney, of Reedham in Norfolk. Edward Paston was a posthumous son of Sir Thomas Paston, and godson of Edward the Sixth, born 1550, died 1630. Edward Paston had six sons, (1) Thomas, (2) William, (3) Clement, (4) Edward, (5) John, (6) Wolstan, who was living in May, 1674. The three daughters were Katherine, Margaret, and Anne; the two first died unmarried, and Anne married Sir Henry Waldegrave. The following letter was addressed by Wolstan Paston to Mr. Drewitt, agent at Oxburgh:

" I have received ye bill of 44^l, and Mr. Philips hath accepted it, to pay it when it will be due. It is to be feared that the proclamation for banishing Priests will be executed by Pursevants, though some say the contrary. Next weeke when the Parliament sits wee shall be better informed, in the meantime I should be glad to heare from you about the seventeene pounds, and five shillings, and remain your affec Friend

"April 23, 1663." "WOLSTAN PASTON.

VOTIVE PICTURE OF THE BEDINGFELD FAMILY KNEELING BENEATH THE MANTLE OF THE BLESSED VIRGIN, PAINTED TO COMMEMORATE THE ESCAPE OF SIR HENRY BEDINGFELD, FIRST BARONET, FROM THE BATTLE OF MARSTON MOOR.

MARGARET LADY BEDINGFELD, WIFE OF FIRST BARONET.

In his will Wolstan Paston left the following legacies: "To Sir Henry Bedingfeld the elder, and to his sonne John, to Edward Paston Esq, and to his brother Clement, to my nephew ffrancis Bedingfeld and to Mary his wife, to Mr. Richard Carrill, and to Mrs. Ellin Waldegrave, twenty shillings apeece to buy them rings for a Memoriall. . . . Dated 2nd day of Sept in the year of our Sovaring Lord King Charles the 2nd of England, Scotland, France, and Ireland, King, defender of the faith the year thirty one."

Sir Henry Bedingfeld, here alluded to as "the elder," was the first Baronet, and nephew by marriage to Wolstan, being Margaret's husband. Sir Henry died in 1684, so this will must have been made before that date. Perhaps Wolstan Paston, being an ardent Royalist, counted "the year of our sovaring Lord King" from the date of the execution of Charles the First in 1649. Thirty-one years from then would bring us to 1680, which might very well be the date of this will. Mr. Richard Carill married a daughter of Sir Henry Bedingfeld's, and she died in 1704. "My nephew ffrancis Bedingfeild" may have been brother of the eleven nuns, who married one of the Pastons of Appleton. "Mrs. Ellin Waldegrave" may have been a niece, daughter of Wolstan's sister, Anne Lady Waldegrave. There is a portrait of Clement Paston at Oxburgh, in the West Wing.

Sir Henry Bedingfeld's eldest daughter, Elizabeth Whetenhall, was one of the beauties of the Court of Charles the Second. She was known as "La Blanche Whetenhall." The following account of her is taken from Count Grammont's Memoirs : "Mrs. Whetenhall was what may be properly called a beauty, entirely English, made up of lilies and roses, of snow and milk as to colour, and of wax with respect to the arms, hands, and neck, but all this without either animation or air; her face was uncommonly pretty, but there was no variety, no change of countenance in it . . . nature had formed her a baby from her infancy, and a baby remained till death the fair Mrs. Whetenhall. Her husband had been destined for the Church, but his elder brother dying just at the time he had gone through his studies of divinity, instead of taking orders he came to England, and took to wife Miss Bedingfeld, the lady of whom we are now speaking. His person was not disagreeable, but he had a serious, contemplative air, very apt to occasion disgust: as for the rest she might boast of having one of the greatest theologists in the kingdom for her husband—he was all day poring over his books, and went to bed soon, in order to rise early. His conversation at table would have been very brisk if Mrs. Whetenhall had been as great a proficient in divinity, or as great a lover of controversy as he was; but being neither learned in the former, nor desirous of the latter, silence reigned at their table, as absolutely as in a refectory."

From the Memoirs it appears further that Mrs. Whetenhall became weary of this secluded life. They lived at Peckham, but although only a day's journey from London, she had never visited the great metropolis. At length, in company with her cousin Miss Hamilton, she went to London, where her head was almost turned with an "excess of contentment and felicity," and "the cabbages and

ELIZABETH BEDINGFELD, MRS. WHETENHALL,

MARY BEDINGFELD, WIFE OF THOS. EYRE, DAUGHTER OF FIRST BARONET.

turkeys at Peckham seemed a thousand times more dreadful to her" after her initiation into the amusements of the town. How she proceeded to Tunbridge Wells with Miss Hamilton, how she took part in all the dissipations of the Court then established there, etc., are all related by the author, who cannot find worse to reproach her with than want of wit, and coldness to her would-be admirers. Her portrait is at Oxburgh, in the west wing passage. Of the other daughters, Frances, married to John Caryll of West Grinstead Place, Esq., had a daughter who entered religion, and was professed at Dunkirk, Dame Mary Magdalene, O.S.B. Mrs. Caryll died September 4th, 1704, aged 68, and was buried in West Grinstead Church, where her monument still exists. Her husband, Mr. John Caryll, was created Baron Caryll by James II. at St. Germains.

The Caryll Family of West Grinstead, Harting, Ladyholt, gave several sons and daughters to the Church, and it is due to the Carylls that the Faith has always been preserved at West Grinstead. Harting was originally the family seat, and they had been settled there from the year 1597.

"John Caryll, who was born during Queen Elizabeth's reign, and who died in the odour of sanctity, made a small provision towards maintaining a priest for ever ' to serve the poor Catholiques of West Grinstead.' His son John was a fervent Catholic and a staunch adherent of his lawful Sovereign, King James II., who sent him to Rome on an important mission to the Holy See. . . . James II. created him

Earl Caryll about 1697, a title which had been offered him some time before he accepted it. . . . He was outlawed in 1694, and his property sequestered by William of Orange and bestowed upon a certain Lord Cutts, who it is believed had been a butcher. . . . The property was afterwards redeemed by the Earl's third brother, Richard, for £6,000. The last of the family, the third Lord Caryll, joined Prince Charles Edward in Italy, and finally died at Dunkirk in poverty and distress. The second Lord Caryll was a friend of Pope, and was imprisoned on two occasions in Horsham Prison, either for recusancy or loyalty to his unfortunate Sovereign. In religion there were eight Benedictine nuns, two Augustinians, two of the Holy Sepulchre (now New Hall), two Benedictine monks, and three Jesuits. We are informed that the family is not yet extinct, but that a lineal descendant of the same name in good circumstances still survives in America."[1]

Of the two nun daughters—Carmelites—Mrs. Anne Bedingfeld died in 1701, having been 31 years in religion. She was professed July 16th, 1670, aged 18, died February 18th, 1701 (Brother Foley[2] gives the date 1700). Margaret, professed August 27th, 1673, aged 27, died Prioress, November 19th, 1714. I have not at the present time any details of Mrs. Eyre's life; her portrait is at Oxburgh, and she appears to have resembled her mother, Dame Margaret. The following members of the Bedingfeld family were in religion about this time: Lucy, fourth Prioress of the English Tere-

---

[1] From Brother Foley, S.J. *Records.*
[2] Brother Foley, S.J., author of *A History of the English Province.*

ANNE BEDINGFELD, DAUGHTER OF FIRST BARONET, (CARMELITE AT LIERRE).

MARGARET BEDINGFELD, DAUGHTER OF FIRST BARONET (A CARMELITE AT LIERRE).

sians at Antwerp—she died of small-pox, January 6th, 1650, aged 36, in the first year of her government; Mary, second Superior of the English Franciscan nuns at Rouen. After governing the house eleven years, she died on March 6, 1670. Amongst the many English who inhabited Brussels was Matthew Bedingfeld, who took up his abode there in 1646. He was grandson of Sir Henry Bedingfeld, Governor of the Tower, and had two daughters (O.S.B.), one at Ghent, and the other at Brussels, and had a son Matthew, a Jesuit. His elder daughter, Margaret, born about 1624, took the habit in 1640 as Sister Thecla, but died during her novitiate, making her vows on her deathbed, February 2, 1642. His daughter Mary was professed at Ghent in 1649, but severe and long illness caused her removal to the monastery at Brussels, where she lived many years, greatly beloved and esteemed, and died Prioress 1685. Her picture used to be at Oxburgh, but it was given by the late Sir Henry (seventh Baronet) to the Benedictine Convent, St. Mary's Abbey, now at East Bergholt. The picture is said to have belonged to the Hon. Charlotte, Lady Bedingfeld. We paid a visit to the convent in 1907, and the Lady Abbess very kindly sent the picture to the parlour for our inspection. Dame Mary is represented in the Benedictine habit, and has a very sweet face. Her father was of Redlingfield, Suffolk. The following necrology of Dame Mary was sent me by Dame Mary Assumpta Vaughan:

"In the year of our Lord 1685, April 21st, in our Monastery of the Glorious Assumption of the Most Blessed Mother of God at Brussels, happily deceased our dear Sister in Christ Dame Mary Bedingfeld. She received the holy Habit of St. Benedict, and was Professed in the Monastery at Ghent in 1649. Having been sent by Superiors to Brussels for the cure of some disease, and lodging in our Monastery, she after her recovery was moved to make petition to remain there instead of returning to Ghent, to which Superiors consenting to, she renewed her holy vow of obedience to the Abbess, Lady Mary Vavasour, September 4, 1661, and there died happily. R.I.P."

The second Baronet succeeded his father in 1684, being then nearly 50 years of age: he came to England with the Duke of Gloucester at the Restoration, and was known as "the great Sir Harry," and famed for his splendid hospitality. "Had not his religion prevented him from filling one of the public stations in his country, no man would have been more popular." Sir Henry's first wife was Anne, only daughter and heiress of Charles Howard, Viscount Andover, afterwards Earl of Berkshire, who died September 19, 1682, and by whom he had no issue. Charles, Earl of Berkshire (who in his father's life-time had summons to divers Parliaments by the title of Lord Howard of Charlton) succeeded his father in 1669, and married Dorothy, second daughter of Thomas, Viscount Savage, by whom he had issue three sons (who died in youth) and two daughters—first, Anne, married to Sir Henry Bedingfeld of Oxburgh in Norfolk, and Elizabeth, who died young. Lord Berkshire's father was Thomas, second son of Thomas, Earl of Suffolk, and was created Earl of Berkshire. For his eminent Parts and Merits he was in the 19th of James I. created first

SIR HENRY BEDINGFELD, SECOND BARONET.

LADY ANNE BEDINGFELD, FIRST WIFE OF THE SECOND BARONET.

Lord Howard of Charlton, and Viscount Andover, and in the 5th of Charles I., advanced to the Degree and Dignity of Earl of Berkshire, and before the end of that reign installed Knight of the Garter. One of the daughters of this Lord Berkshire, Elizabeth, married John Dryden, the Poet Laureate.[1] Sir Harry married secondly Elizabeth, youngest daughter of Sir John Arundell of Lanherne, in Cornwall, Bart., by whom he had a son, Henry Arundell, his successor, and three daughters—viz., 1, Elizabeth, who died young of the small-pox; 2, Margaret, wife of Sir John Jerningham of Cossey, in Norfolk, Bart., and 3rd, Frances—her portrait hangs in the big saloon, Oxburgh, and she has been known to successive generations as "the pretty lady"—who married Sir Francis Anderton of Lostock, in Lancashire, Bart., and died without issue. Elizabeth, Lady Bedingfeld, died at the early age of 35, leaving her children in the nursery, the eldest, Elizabeth, being five years old, and the little son and heir aged one year. On her monument is the following:

"Beneath this monument is interred the most virtuous and pious Lady Elizabeth, youngest daughter of Sir John Arundell, of Lanhern in Cornwall, and second wife to Sir Henry Bedingfeld of Oxburgh, Knt. and Bart., who in the 35th year of her age departed this life on the 13th of April, 1690—leaving an only son and three daughters." There is a "Memorandum Book" at Oxburgh written by Sir Harry, giving the following interesting details:

[1] This account is taken from a contemporary Peerage at Oxburgh, dated 1709.

"My first wife was a comely well-featured person, of great memorie and good will, very virtuous and charitable, she presently grew very fatt, and was sick severall yeares of ye gout: dyed at ye age 34." Of his second marriage he wrote: "May 3, 1684, I married Elizabeth Arundell, Daughter of Sir John Arundell of Lanherne in Cornwall, she dyed at Oxborrow April 13, 1690, and lyes buryed just by my first wife, she left me four children, and dyed with child.

"The first child was borne 25 February, 1685, in Bow Streete London, and being a girl was christened Elizabeth, Lady Belling Godmother, my Brother John Godfather.

"The second was borne 3rd March, 1686, London, being a girle was christened Margarett, Sir John Arundell Godfather, and my Mother Godmother.

"The third was borne 14th November, 1687, London, being a girle was christened Frances, Sir Richard Belling Godfather, Sister Caryell Godmother.

"The forth was borne 13th of April, 1689, London, being a Boy was christened Henry Arundell, Sir John Arundell Godfather, Sister Eyre Godmother.

"My second wife was tall and well shaped. Browne haire, but fine complexion, and handsome, she had excellent partes and great sense, but by long and many yeares of sickness was affected with ye spleen and vapours, which was ye cause of her short life, dying at ye age of 35.

"When I came first with my wife, ye Lady Anne, to live here [Oxburgh] I was £450 in debt, and I was forced to repair this house, and all my tenants houses, which put me into debt . . . at least £3,500, which I

LADY BEDINGFELD (*née* ARUNDELL), WIFE OF SECOND BARONET.

TOMB OF 'THE GREAT SIR HARRY' AND HIS TWO WIVES.
(*In the Bedingfeld Chapel, Oxburgh.*)

paid most of it by bargains I made, what my Uncle Paston left, and by £1,500 I had of my brother John's portion. But for that £1,500 I am like to bee a great sufferer, by reason I agreed with my father in consideration of ye £1,500 to lett my brother John enjoye Ashill during my mother's life, from ye death of my father—soe that I have already repaid since my father's death £2,700 in consideration of £1,500. And in all likelyhood I may pay it many yeares, which as times are has half ruined me. When I consider well my expenses, I find I have spent a great deal of money since 1666, and I have for my justification the obligation of maintaining my first wife according to her quality, which I did to gaine my Lady Berkshire's favour. And then it is to be considered, I had not till my father's death six hundred pounds to live on, soe considering how I lived, and what vast expense I was at in repairing houses, I wonder I did not run further in debt. And since my father's death I have all ye charge of the families upon me, and I daresay I never received £1,000 a year, Ashill being deducted, Shingham to my Brother Edward, and a rent charge of £120 per annum to my mother out of Cavenham, are considerable matters out of ye estate; I must alsoe say something for myselfe, for spending my last wife's portion, being £4,000, I lived in London in hopes of getting great matters at Court, as I was promessed. And alsoe my house being burnt, gave my wife small encouragement to live here, soe that in supplying ye house with furniture that was burnt, and making the house habitable, it cost me £1,000, and £4,000 I laid out in purchases, soe I conclude I spent £2,000 in expectation of great matters which proved nothing but 'Court holy water'—and since the Revolution I find I have directly run in debt. . . ." (Here follows a list of payments).

It is said that the heavy renaissance furniture now at Oxburgh was brought by Sir Henry from abroad to replace what was burnt by Cromwell's Roundheads. In addition to his other expenses, Sir Henry was obliged to pay £20 a month for non-attendance at the parish church, and if a priest visited him both the priest and Sir Henry were liable to imprisonment. Jesuit Fathers served the Oxburgh Mission from the time of James II. until 1795. Father Pordage, S.J., was chaplain at Oxburgh in 1683, when he first came there; he died in 1736, at the advanced age of 88, and was buried in the Bedingfeld Chapel attached to the parish church. He thus lived at Oxburgh during the lives of the three first Baronets, and was succeeded by Fathers Philip Cartaret, Richard Clough, Thomas Hawkins, and Thomas Angier. There was a portrait of Father Pordage at Oxburgh (mentioned by Charlotte, Lady Bedingfeld), but so far it has not been identified. It is the more difficult to discover because probably he was painted in secular dress. The portrait of Lady Anne, Sir Henry's first wife, hangs on the West Wing staircase. She is represented in a red satin dress and a blue mantle edged with gold; she has dark hair and eyes, and is of stately appearance.

In the "Memorandum Book" from which I have quoted, Sir Henry wrote the following particulars of the Countess of Berkshire (Lady Anne's mother): "Lady Berkshire dyed on Sunday ye 6th day of

FRANCES BEDINGFELD, LADY ANDERTON, DAUGHTER OF THE SECOND BARONET.

MARGARET BEDINGFELD, LADY JERNINGHAM,
DAUGHTER OF SECOND BARONET.

December, 1698, aboute halfe an houre after four a clocke in ye afternoon, and was caryed on ye fryday following to New Elms in Oxfordshire to be buryed." Lady Berkshire appointed her son-in-law, Sir Henry, residuary legatee as follows in the copy of her will. "As for concerning ye Residue and Remainder of all my estate, etc., etc., I give and devize ye same unto ye said Sir Henry Bedingfeld as a marke and token of ye Respect I bear him for his great kindness and affection unto my dear Daughter, his late deceased Wife. This twenty-fourth day of December, and fourth year of our sovorayne Lord, King James ye Second, and year of our Lord God, 1688." Sir Henry added this further note: "My Lady Berkshire was a person of great honour, and was very kind to me at all times, or else I must have been a beggar." An interesting personality of this period of family history was Mr. Thomas Marwood (tutor to young Henry Arundell Bedingfeld); he has left a Journal and other papers. The Journal begins on Tuesday, August 22, 1699, when Marwood and his pupil left Oxburgh and went abroad. Sir Henry's three daughters, Elizabeth, Margaret, and Frances, had already gone, and were staying with their aunts, Margaret and Anne Bedingfeld, who were nuns at the English Carmelite convent at Lierre, where the good Canon had died in 1680. Pictures of the two nuns and their great uncle "hung and still hang on the walls of their Norfolk home, an indication of the strong bond of affection which existed between the various members of the family. The separation of the cloister brought no division or oblivion to the children of Dame Margaret, and her grand-children

G

would have known their aunts' faces before they actually met them." Henry Arundell was ten years old when he left home, and is nearly always called the Esq. in the Journal. In addition to Mr. Marwood, the Esq. was accompanied by Father Pordage and the nurse, Mrs. Masterson. They stayed first at Ipswich, then took boat for Harwich, and arrived at Antwerp on August 27th, and Lierre was reached by September 8th. Here the Esq. met his sisters and aunts, visits were exchanged with the Governor's lady, and Sir Henry joined his family on September 25th by way of Calais and Dunkirk. They all paid a visit to the " Biggainage of Lyre, a neat enclosure and church dedicated to St. Margaret, about 150 Religious in it." St. Teresa's day was celebrated " with great splendour " by the Carmelite nuns, and on October 19th Sir Henry took all the children to Brussels in a large travelling waggon. The young ladies went to the " Louvainesses " (Augustinian nuns), who were paid 200 florins for the first quarter; there were also dancing and music masters. All Souls' day was solemnly kept at Brussels, " and the bells rang almost all night to remind people to pray." The Esq. was placed at the Jesuit College. Sir Henry was occasionally troubled with the gout; he frequently dined with Lord Ailesbury, sometimes taking the children with him. He also went to the play, and he moved into new quarters, " Aux trois Fontaines, Mons. Jacques." In the midst of this agreeable life, the Bedingfelds were suddenly visited by a great sorrow: the eldest girl, Elizabeth, was stricken by small-pox, and her two sisters were hastily sent back to Lierre to escape the contagion.

The illness had run its course for ten days, and Marwood wrote, " Mrs. Elizabeth gave all the signs of doing well "—but the following day came the sad entry : " In the morn her feavor began to grow upon her, and to talk idle. . . . Afternoon she was worse, and at night the D^r told me she was in Danger, and therefore must dispose her for the end. I sent for Fr. Cotton, who was with her most of the night. And at five she fell a sleep, ab^t $\frac{1}{2}$ seaven waked in her Agonie, and ab^t 8·in the morning—Thursday, 24 Dec., she dyed like an Angel, R.I.P., about $\frac{1}{4}$ past 8. That night I saw her decently interred in ye Chappell vault belonging to ye Religious, but privately because her Decease was not to be Knowne."

This secrecy had to be observed on account of the penal laws, then lately passed in England, which made it unlawful for a Catholic parent to send his children " beyond the seas " to be educated in " Popery." For the same reason the Esq. about this time took the name of Nelson, and was so called by Mr. Marwood in the Journal. In an old copy of Virgil in the Oxburgh library, the name " Nelson " appears on the fly-leaf, with the following explanation written at a later period : " Henry Arundell Bedingfeld, who at school was called Nelson on account of the Test Laws."

After this the Esq. fell ill, and was tenderly nursed by Mr. Marwood. At first it was feared that he too would develop the dreaded small-pox, but fortunately he did not, though he seems to have had a great deal of fever. On his recovery he was moved to Lierre in a coach, accompanied by his nurse, Mrs. Masterson, and his tutor. Sir Henry left for Antwerp in the

February following these events, *en route* for England; and in May, Margaret and Frances, accompanied by their nurse, left for Dunkirk to continue their education at the convent there, the Lady Abbess, Mary Caryll, being a connection of the Bedingfelds. The Esq. (with Mr. Marwood) accompanied his sisters as far as Antwerp. From Antwerp they went to Bornhem, and on August 4th the Esq. made his First Communion. Sir Henry wrote for his eldest girl Margaret, and she returned to England with Mrs. Masterson, and the Esq. and Marwood were ordered to start for France. There were many English Catholics at this time living in the Low Countries, and amongst those encountered by the Bedingfelds, mention is made of Carylls, Jernegans, Stanleys, Tasburghs, Huddlestons, Southwells, Pastons, Copleys, &c.

"30 Dec. 1700. At night we got to Boulogne, which is a pretty old town fortifyed with walls and towers à l'antique, and separate from ye Basse Ville where we lay at Monsr Gaillards at ye angel. For our meat we went to ye Rotisseur, where we had a Capon larded, a Rabbit larded, a Pigeon and two greenes for 45 sous, all ready drest." Arrived in Paris they visited all the principal places, "Ye Pontneuf, Louvre, Thuillerys, Jardin de Luxemburgh, Ye Invalides (which is capable of 6,000 beds), Palais Royall, much like ye Exchange and Westminster Hall." They went to the "Carmelite Convent of ye Incarnation," where Madame de la Valière was then a Religious. They visited Mrs. Throckmorton and Mrs. Wheatenhall (the latter a cousin of the Esq.) "at ye Hôtel d'Estrade," and took coach for Versailles with Mr. Eyre and Mr. Paston (Dom Clement Paston), and at Versailles they saw "Ye King of France, ye Dauphin, Monsr the Duke de Chartres and Duchesse de Burgogne all at supper about 10 at night."

"Wed. 19th. We took coach for La Flesche, 52 leagues from Paris, at 8 morn, accompanied by R. P. de Pré and P. Contancine, who was going for China with Mr. de Fontenay. We dined at Palesseau, 4 leagues from Paris, a poor village, and supped at Bonelle, 4 leagues farther.

"Thurs. 20th. We dined at Guêt de Lauret, 6 leagues, where ye Dutchesse de la Ferté and her daughter ye Marquise de Mirepoix (a prodigious fat woman) came into our chamber to speak with P. Contancine. We came to Chartres that night, a neat wal'd towne, the church celebrated for Beauty, 4 leagues from Guêt de Lauret, and there we lay.

"Frid. 21. We dined at Heliers, 6 leagues from Chartres; a poor village. We sup'd this night at Les Autels, 5 leagues, and came in late, at 9 at night, an ordinary village.

"Saturd. 22. We dined at Pont de Veni, a low village, at that time much overflowed with water; and came in at 3 o'clock, the wheel being mended by the way. And there we stay'd till 9 night, because ye next stage was very bad way; and we stay'd for ye Benefit of ye Moon, and to make our horses in good heart, for we had a league in a Rapid Water and dreadful way beside, before we came to Conary, 4 leagues off.

"Sunday, 23. We came about 3 in the morning to Conary, when I put ye Esq. to bed, and lay downe only myself. We heard P. Contancine's Masse in ye parish church about 7, and then took a good breakfast, intending only a collation at Mans, a neat Citty 5 leagues off. And at night we came to Gévelaer, about 4 leagues off, but excellent way—and there we lay.

"Monday, 24. We came to La Flesche by 10 o'clock in ye morning—bad way mostly, and din'd together at ye 4 Vents, where I took up my lodging till ye Saturday following."

The Esq. now entered upon his course of study, and remained at the college four years. His natural gifts and steady application resulted in a thoroughly successful school career, which must have been a source of comfort to his father.

"Tuesday, Jan. 25. I was visited by Mr. Farjet, and went to Lord Waldegrave's, who invited us to dinner and supper. We also saw Mr. Hescott [Father Thos. Haskett, S.J.], who introduced us to J. de la Ferté [Père de la Ferté, S.J.], who received us most kindly.

"Wed. Jan. 26. Père Contancine tooke his leave of us (recommending me to Père Hirvien and de la More). We saw all ye College which is beautifull and stately, built by Hen 4, whose Heart with his Queen, Mary de Medicis is there, and therefore called ye Royall College. I writ this day to Sir Henry, Mr. Luton, Mr. Paston, Mrs. Frances. Dined at home.

"Friday, Feb. 18. Dyed Mrs. Anne Bedingfeld at Lyre ætat 50. Rel. 31.

"Sunday, April 3. Mrs. Smith went for Paris by ye way of Orleans. I writ to Sir Henry. And about

2 afternoon Lord Walgrave, Mr. Widrington, Mr. Acland (alias Horsey), the Esq. and myself accompanied her and Mr. Skelton to Tours, which is 14 leagues off, in order to see the country. We came to Lud that night 4 leagues east, and lay at Notre Dame, Bellcrits, and bespoke a Periwig of Mr. Fouchier there. There is a neat chateau belonging to the Duke de Rochloire, who is now about 42 years old, and has never been in it since he was eight years old. Yet it is a neat, regular, and strong building, well furnisht, and a noble wald Park, and good stables, a very deep ditch wald without, and a brave home work (just against the River which runs below it) now made a neat garden with balustres round it.

"Monday 4. We past thro Chateau which is 3 leagues farther, and din'd at Sovigné, a small village belonging to Mad^{me} de Valière, as does the noble wood of Beaujour nere it, and the château of the same name now given to her daughter who is married to the Prince de Conti. And that night arrived at Tours, 10 leagues from Lude, where we lay at the Galaire royale.

"Tuesday 5. We went about the Towne (Mrs. Smith leaving us nere 9 ith morne). Saw the noble Mall the length of the Towne, above ½ a league long, just under the Town walls, south next the Towne, in a strait line. Then we saw their silk Manufacture, the famous Clock of Tours in the Cathedrall of St. Gassieu. We went up the Towre of it, 300 steps high, and saw all the beautifull situation of the Towne, and fine houses round about. . . . From the Tower might be seen the fine chateau of Chaumont nere Blois, on the East, and the Benedictine Monastery of Marmotier, the finest in

Europe, on ye north side of the Loyre. . . . There is about 16 Parishes in the Town and about as many monasterys in and about it. We cald at the Jesuites and were invited to dinner by P. ——, but we took horse about 11 and came about 6 at night to the Ecu d'or at Chateau, where we lay. . . .

"Wed. 6 April. We went in the morn to see the Iron Forge which is very fine, all the bellows and hammers of 900 weight turned by water like an overshot mill. There is a Verriere not far off, but we went not to see it, but took horse about 11, came to Lud about 4 and din'd, and about 6 took horse for La Flesche, where we arrived safe about 9, ye Esq safe and well."

This was the first of several journeys and excursions undertaken from La Flesche. On the 23rd May they heard the news that King William was "desperately sick," and that "Jamaco was almost destroyed by an earthquake." The next day they started for Angers. In September of this year is the following entry:

"Mond. 19. We had the news that King James dyed the 16 Instant, at about 4 afternoon, and that his body was ordered to be deposited with the English monkes at Paris, till he should be buryed with his ancestors."

"7th March 1702. Yesterday was Publish[d] by Sound of Trumpet an Ordonnance du Roy for all English, Scotch and Irish, from 18 to 50 that were in France, and not in Employ; to take Service in ye Army on peine of being treated as Deserters.

"Thursd. 31. We had the Acc[t] of the Prince of

Orange's death said to be Thursday the 23 Instant but proved on St Joseph's ye 19."

On the 11th April they set out for Mans, and were kindly received there by the Bishop, who lent them his coach to see the town. The following day,

"Wed. 12. At 11 in the morn we set out of Mans for Alenson the first Towne of Normandy, where we Arrived at 7 evening, 10 Leagues. Bayted at Beaumont, 6 Leagues from Mans."

From Alençon to Barenton they arrived at Courti, and took a guide to Mont St. Michel, and lodged at "Ye Chapeau Rouge." Here they saw "all the Raretys of the Castle and Convent which is situate nere 4 or 500 foot fro the sea, which surrounds the Rock at high water. And has about 70 houses, all walled in, but on the north side where the hill is a Precipice. The Rock is about ½ a mile in compass, and the Prior is Lord and Cap^n of the Castle, the Place is much visited by Devout Persons, and we are told that some Lordships about, have the Custome that an Heir cant Inherit, till he have visited St. Michaels."

From thence they went to St. Malo, and lodged at the "Cheval Blanc," called on the Benedictines and saw over the fortifications, and after a further tour in Brittany, returned safely to La Flesche. The following month they started on another excursion, halting first at Saumure.

"Mond. 5 June. We visited the Towne wch is small and has a good Wall, but else nothing noted but for being a Nursury of Heresy, the Hugonots had scholes here, but now all destroyed. . . ."

They then took horse for Chinon, and called at a "famous Monastery of Nuns," the Lady Abbess being a sister of Mdme. de Montespan. Then to Richelieu, where they came to a "Fine House of ye Duke of Orleans . . . where is adjoining a Noble Chappel called La Sainte Chapelle, from the Many Curious Reliques there kept, all which I had toucht by my reliquary."

The following year came news of the death of the Esq's grandmother.

"16 Feb. 1703. I had a letter from Mrs Southwell with the news of the death of my Lady Bedingfeld, who dyed ye 14th Jan."

On Palm Sunday of this year, Mr. Marwood and his pupil went into Retreat, and after a few days Mr. Marwood "made a sort of General Confession." On the feast of St. Ignatius in the following July,

"Afternoon Mr Nelson being with his book in his hand, alone in the Berceau after dinner, he told me that evening that he then heard a voice as he thought say, 'Mr Nelson, Mr Nelson,' wch gave him a little Apprehension, but he past it over, as I did, when he told it me."

The Journal ends on the 24th Sept. 1703. It has been published word for word, with learned and copious notes, by the Rev. Father Pollen, S.J., for the Catholic Records Series, and from this we learn a great many interesting details of the persons and places mentioned by Marwood and of the College of La Flesche. In addition to the very excellent tuition given, there was every facility for outdoor games, such as football, tennis, shooting, riding and swimming; and in all this, the Fathers must have been far in advance of the age they lived in.

The following year "the great Sir Harry" died, but it is probable that his son stayed on at College for another year, as he was only fifteen when he succeeded to the baronetcy. The following paper written by Marwood is at Oxburgh. It is an epitaph composed by the good man, and designed for the tomb of his friend and patron.

"The Copy of the Epitaph Mr Edward Bedingfeld desired me to make for Sir Henry Bedingfeld's Tomb, and which I sent him: but it was not, it seems, liked by him.

"I.H.S.

"Here lyes the body of Sir Henry Bedingfeld of Oxburgh, ye 15 Knight and 2nd Bart (in a direct descent) of his Family, whose Personage, accomplishments and good Qualitys rendered him eminently Knowne and esteemed in his Life, and Lamented at his Death. Hee was of Personage Noble, Aimable and agreeable; of Abord easy; of Conversation Pleasant. His Religion and Loyalty he rec^d from a long and uninterrupted Line of Ancestors, as a Sacred Depôt, which he left untainted to his young children. (For he was married young to the onely daughter of the Earl of Berkshire, by whom he had no Issue. After her death to the eldest daughter of Sir John Arundell, by whom he had one onely son and 3 daughters, the eldest of which dyed at Bruxels in his lifetime.) Hospitality, an hereditary virtue of his Family, he maintained and Improved even to envy.

He was valued, and valuable, in the different devoirs of his Life—being a good Friend, a good Neighbour, a good Husband, a good Master, a good Father, and had all the Qualitys that make a good and compleat Gentleman, without the least alloy of Fault: he quitted this Life in Christian hopes of a better, Sept 14 1704, aged 60 and odde years.

Requiescat in Pace.

Designed by his gratefull Servant Thos Marwood."

There are two portraits of "Sir Harry" at Oxburgh. The first as a young man, handsome and spirited, in flowing wig and armour; the second taken in middle age, very stately of aspect.

It is good to know that the worthy tutor lived long enough to see his beloved pupil attain his majority, and we may feel sure that the tie between them was of the most affectionate nature.[1]

The hopes of the family were now centred on the young heir, so sadly deprived of his father at an age

---

[1] The following paper gives us the date of Mr. Marwood's death.
"Nov. 1, 1718.—Received then of Sir Henry Bedingfeld ye sum of sixteen shillings and eight pence for ye mortuary and ye Buriall of ye late Mr. Marwood,—I say Recd by me
Cha Parkin."
(Mr. Parkin was Rector of Oxburgh and an antiquary).
Mr. Marwood wrote out the following list of Anniversaries in his prayer book.
Sir Henry Bedingfeld of Beckhall dyed Feb. 24, 1684–5.
The Lady Anne Bedingfeld dyed Sept. 19th, 1682.
The Lady Elizabeth Bedingfeld dyed April 13th, 1689.
Captain William Bedingfeld dyed Jan. ye 30th, 1685,–6.
Mr. John Bedingfeld (ye Uncle), dyed Feb. 18th, 1685-6.
Mr. Jo Bedingfeld (Wickmer), dyed Aug. 9th, 1693. R.I.P.

SIR HENRY BEDINGFELD, SECOND BARONET.

SIR HENRY ARUNDELL BEDINGFELD, THIRD BARONET.

when he most needed his care and guidance. Sir Henry Arundell Bedingfeld seems to have amply upheld the traditions of his race, though we possess very scanty information about him. I have come across only two small scraps of his handwriting amongst the Oxburgh papers: two short letters, one to his sister on the death of his wife, and one to his son Edward. There are a good many of his letters in the British Museum, and they have been published by Father Pollen in the collection already alluded to. Amongst these are several letters to the Duke of Newcastle, but the most interesting relate to the detection of one Archibald Bower (an apostate Jesuit), in which Sir Henry played a most important part, and according to Father Pollen, by his "tact managed to enlist on his side the services of some of the most eminent literati then in the Anglican Communion." There is an old document called "Pedigrees of the Bedingfelds" which gives this account: "Sir Henry dyed, leaving one son, ye present Sir Henry, but lately arrived at his majority, and who, ye advantage of a noble stature and proportions, a carefull education in learning and exercises, and those polishes by travell in foreign Courts, give great hopes he will be a worthy descendant to such deserving Ancestors."

We are reminded that the persecuting laws against Catholics were in full force by an Oxburgh paper entitled "License from the Justices, Aug. 10, 1713, for Sir Henry Bedingfeld to go from home for a month."

"Whereas Sir Henry Bedingfeld of Oxburgh, Bart., being a Recusant, and confined to the usual place of his abode, or within the compass of five miles from the same, and whereas it has been represented to us on the part of the said Sir Henry Bedingfeld that he has very necessary and urgent business which does require his attendance at this time, and whereas ye said Sir Henry Bedingfeld has made oath before us of the truth of the same, and that he will not make any causeless stay from his said place of habitation. We therefore four of his Majesty's Justices of Peace for the said County upon examination taken by us of the premisses, do give this our License to the said Sir Henry Bedingfeld to travel out of the precincts or compass of five miles from the place of his abode limited by the statute at all times from the 13 of this instant August until the thirteenth of September following, by which time he is to return again to his place of abode at the Parish of Oxburgh aforesaid.

"Given under our hand and seales this 10th of August, 1713.

"H. Partridge, Dep. Lieut. I Do Assent to this License."

Sir Henry married August, 1719, the Lady Elizabeth Boyle, eldest daughter of Charles, late Earl of Burlington. In a letter to the Duke of Newcastle, dated 1743 (Catholic Records), Sir Henry, writing on the occasion of a Proclamation against the "Papists," asks for protection from the Government, and goes on to say: "It would besides be very hard that Lady Betty should be deprived of horses to carrye her to church, or to visitt her neighbours at a distance, and not in a manner suitable to her quality."

From this Father Pollen concludes the lady was a

LADY ELIZABETH BEDINGFELD, WIFE OF THIRD BARONET.

Protestant, and the surmise is, I think, confirmed by a book of Protestant devotions (lately arrived at Oxburgh amongst Mr. Felix Bedingfeld's collection), and containing Lady Betty's name on the fly-leaf. She has left a list of her children with their god-parents.

"The first was a son dead born May 28, 1720.

"The second a son born August 28, 1721; he died soon after.

"The third Elizabeth, born Novr 7, 1722.

"The fourth Henry, born Octr 27, 1723. He died Septr 6, 1732.

"The fifth Charles, born Octr 17, 1724; he died at 2 months old.

"The sixth Mary, born Septr 27, 1725; at the 7th month she died.

"The seventh Richard, born Sept[r] 14, 1726.

"The eighth Edward, born Feb. 2, 1730.

The Godfathers and Godmothers.

"To Betty, Lady Thanet, Lady Dowr Burlington, Lord Burlington.

"To Harry, Lord Burlington, Lord Carleton, Lady Burlington.

"To Charles, the Duke of Queensberry, Lord Wilmington, Lady Dalkeith.

"To Richard, Lord Litchfield, Mr. Boyle, Lady Bruce.

"To Edward, Lord Bruce, Sir John Swinburne, Lady Litchfield.

"The above was wrote by my mother. Rich[d] Bedingfeld."

In such a Catholic house as Oxburgh, we are not surprised to find a souvenir of the great Bishop Challoner (who on his departure from Douay College came on the English Mission in 1730). It is an autograph letter addressed to "Esq. Widdrington." One of the Widdringtons was at "La Flesche" with Sir Henry, and very intimate with him, which may account for this letter having found its way to Oxburgh.

"Dear Sir,

"Excuse these lines which come from one who is your hearty well wisher, tho' entirely a stranger to you: this being not any humble petition for myself or for any other, but for your own dear Soul, which God has made immortal to his own image, and for which Christ died. Oh! take pity, dear Sir, of this Soul of yours, which is hanging over a dismal precipice, every moment in danger of being plunged into a miserable eternity. Think, dear Sir, whilst you have time, and return without delay from these husks of swine, that can never satisfy your immortal Soul, to your true Father, who will receive you with open arms, and restore you to his mercy. Otherwise, the Sword of his justice, which always hangs over the head of unrepenting Sinners, will quickly fall upon you and cut you off, in your sins, which God in his mercy forbid. Tis the prayer of

"Your affectionate humble Servant in Christ,

"R. CHALLONER.

"To Esquire Widdrington."

The Hon. Charlotte, Lady Bedingfeld, wrote an account of Lady Elizabeth Bedingfeld as follows:

"23rd Lady Bedingfeld, Lady Elizabeth Boyle. This lady was the wife of Sir Henry Arundell Bedingfeld, 3rd Baronet. She married August 28, 1719, and her eldest Son was born the year following, at her Parents house at Chiswick. Her father was Charles, Earl of Burlington, and her mother was Julia, daughter and heir of Henry Noel, 2nd son to Edward, Viscount Campden, who died 1677. Her paternal Grandfather and Grandmother were, Charles, Lord Clifford, who died in his father's life time, 1694, and Jane, daughter and co-heir to Wm Duke of Somerset. Lady Elizabeth's sisters were (1) Juliana, Lady Bruce, (2) Lady Jane Boyle, who lived on Turnham Green, and died unmarried (her portrait is at Oxburgh.) (3) The Countess of Shannon. Her brother, Richard Earl of Burlington, left an only daughter, his sole heir, who married the Duke of Devonshire, and was mother to the present Duke (ob 1811) and to the late Dutchy of Portland—by this marriage, all the Burlington property passed into the Duke of Devonshire's family, and nothing to the Bedingfelds but some indifferent views of Chiswick Gardens and some curious table linen. Lady Elizabeth Bedingfeld was a woman of merit, but not so happy in the married state as her predecessor, Margaret Paston. She had a great many children, and had the misfortune of losing her eldest son, Henry, at ten years old, and several others in infancy. For the last years of her life she never left her apartments, being afflicted with a dropsy, which rendered her unwieldly, but she had been remarkably active and nimble. An old man at Oxburgh, who had been her servant when a youth, told me that when he went to announce dinner to her, she walked so quick after him that he could hardly get down in time to open the doors for her without running. She was remarkably fond of dogs, and had several always in her dressing-room. She died November 25th, 1750, and lies in Oxburgh Church. She only left three children, two sons and one daughter."

Lady Betty's Chapel, a small ruin with a fine Norman arch, and Lady Betty's Wood, still exist at Oxburgh. By her portraits she appears to have had dark hair, and to be pleasing rather than handsome. Sir Henry wrote the following letter to his sister on the death of his wife:

"Dear Sister, I am extreamly obliged to you for the share you are please to take in ye generall Calamity that has lately befallen to us. I have endeed lost a most valuable Wife, and one who would have been a comfort to me in my old age. God's will be done, and we must make a virtue of necessity. All here present their affec humble service to you, and I beg mine to Mr Masson.

"I am Dear Sister yr affec brother and humble servant
"HENRY BEDINGFELD.

"Oxburgh, 10th Dec 1751."

The other letter at Oxburgh written by Sir Henry was endorsed by his second son Edward, thus:

JACOBITE GLASS WITH PORTRAIT OF PRINCE CHARLIE.
DISCOVERED RECENTLY AT OXBURGH BY MR. CHARLES
EDWARD JERNINGHAM.

" Dated April 2nd 1754.

" My Brother's Letter from Bath, concerning the same affair, was dated March 31st, 1754.

" I am sorry to tell you, that the Lawyers upon examining the title deeds of this Estate of ye Late Lady Burlington, finds that it falls to Lady Jane, the Speaker's eldest son, and my eldest son, Mr. Biddulph (who is in town) had it confirmed to him yesterday the same thing, by Mr Maire. How Sr Anthony Abdy came to be so mistaken as he was, when he wrote me ye letter I shewd you, I cannot conceive, but now he ownes his error. I beg my most affec Service to my Lady Swinburne, and am D^r S^r yr affec father and hum^{ble} servant,

"HENRY BEDINGFELD.

" The letters will not be admitted to be frank'd after next thursday, nor till the parlmt meets again at Westminster."

Sir Henry's second son Edward was said to be his favourite, and it was evidently a disappointment to him to find that Edward would not inherit under his grandmother's will. Sir Henry survived his wife 9 years, and died at Oxburgh on July 15th, 1760, aged 71. He left two sons—Richard, who succeeded him as fourth baronet, Edward, and a daughter Elizabeth. Edward married Miss Mary Swinburne of Capheaton, Elizabeth married Mr. Charles Biddulph of Sussex.

END OF PART II.

NOTES.

Note I. Some references to the family in public records earlier than the fourteenth century.

(i) Before A.D. 1138. King Stephen confirmed to the Priors of Eye the tithes of Peter de Bedingfeld.

(ii) 5 Richard I. Adam de Bedingfeld was fined 5 marcs and gave 12 sureties for the payment.

(iii) A.D. 1198. Adam de Bedingfeld paid 20 shillings not to cross the sea.

(iv) A.D. 1200. Adam de Bedingfeld fined 50 marcs.

(v) A.D. 1203. Adam de Bedingfeld mentioned in connection with the Manor of Tickhall.

(vi) A.D. 1216. The Sheriff of Norfolk and Suffolk was directed to seize the land and body of Adam de Bedingfeld, but in the same year, after the death of King John, the Sheriff was ordered to restore his land to Adam who had returned to his allegiance (Close Roll, vol. i. p. 334).

(vii) A.D. 1225. Adam de Bedingfeld brought a suit against de Brackley.

(viii) A.D. 1259. Adam sued Wm. de Fleming concerning pasturage on the common pasture in Bedingfeld.

(ix) A.D. 1270. Adam fined.

Note II. Page 49 — Sandringham. "Sandringham Manor pays to the Lady Margaret Bedingfeld and to her heirs for ever the yearly Rent Charge of forty pounds" (Marwood's Account Book).

Note III. Page 64—Fald course. Fald-course (*i.e.*, fold-course) was the name given in some places to *faldage*, an old privilege by which the Lord of the Manor could set up folds in which the tenants were obliged to put their sheep. The following extract from Marwood's Account Book relates to a fald-course at Oxburgh :

Aprill 2 Anno 1688
Oxburgh Fold Course
Antiently I presume there was no body did dispute with the Lord about the Number or Quality of his Flock; or their Manner and time for Feed. The Lords being too Equitable than to Oppresse their Tenants.

And the Tenants too Respectfull than to dare contest with their Lords; yet the Spirit of Rebellion diffusing itself, in the Long War between the King, Charles the First, and the Long Parliament, In which Time the Lord of Oxburgh Sir Henry Bedingfeld (together with his Sons etc) lead by the Principalls of Conscience and Honour, took their Sovereign's Part, for which their Persons were Imprisoned, and their Estates Sequestred; Then the Townesmen of Oxburgh thought it proper to dispute with the Fermours of this manner, and to pretend to abridge the Sheepswalke which the Fermours (the Lords being absent or Imprisoned) would not hazard a Suit to Defend. .... Tis not therefore Impertinent to make some observations of the Sheepswalke, as well to guide the future Servants of the Lord, as to preserve ye knowledge of the Customs have been used in my time."